Top Careers in Two Years

Food, Agriculture, and Natural Resources

Titles in the *Top Careers in Two Years* Series

Top Careers in Two Years

Food, Agriculture, and Natural Resources

By Scott Gillam

Ferguson Publishing
An imprint of Infobase Publishing

Top Careers in Two Years
Food, Agriculture, and Natural Resources

Ferguson
An imprint of Infobase Publishing
132 West 31st Street
New York, NY 10001

ISBN-13: 978-0-8160-6896-8
ISBN-10: 0-8160-6896-8

Library of Congress Cataloging-in-Publication Data

Top careers in two years.
     v. cm.
   Includes index.
   Contents: v. 1. Food, agriculture, and natural resources / by Scott Gillam — v. 2. Construction and trades / Deborah Porterfield — v. 3. Communications and the arts / Claire Wyckoff — v. 4. Business, finance, and government administration / Celia W. Seupal — v. 5. Education and social services / Jessica Cohn — v. 6. Health care, medicine, and science / Deborah Porterfield — v. 7. Hospitality, human services, and tourism / Rowan Riley — v. 8. Computers and information technology / Claire Wyckoff — v. 9. Public safety, law, and security / Lisa Cornelio, Gail Eisenberg — v. 10. Manufacturing and transportation — v. 11. Retail, marketing, and sales / Paul Stinson.
   ISBN-13: 978-0-8160-6896-8 (v. 1 : hc : alk. paper)
   ISBN-10: 0-8160-6896-8 (v. 1 : hc : alk. paper)
   ISBN-13: 978-0-8160-6897-5 (v. 2 : hc. : alk. paper)
   ISBN-10: 0-8160-6897-6 (v. 2 : hc. : alk. paper)
   ISBN-13: 978-0-8160-6898-2 (v. 3 : hc : alk. paper)
   ISBN-10: 0-8160-6898-4 (v. 3 : hc : alk. paper)
   ISBN-13: 978-0-8160-6899-9 (v. 4 : hc : alk. paper)
   ISBN-10: 0-8160-6899-2 (v. 4 : hc : alk. paper)
   ISBN-13: 978-0-8160-6900-2 (v. 5 : hc : alk. paper)
   ISBN-10: 0-8160-6900-X (v. 5 : hc : alk. paper)
   ISBN-13: 978-0-8160-6901-9 (v. 6 : hc : alk. paper)
   ISBN-10: 0-8160-6901-8 (v. 6 : hc : alk. paper)
   ISBN-13: 978-0-8160-6902-6 (v. 7 : hc : alk. paper)
   ISBN-10: 0-8160-6902-6 (v. 7 : hc : alk. paper)
   ISBN-13: 978-0-8160-6903-3 (v. 8 : hc : alk. paper)
   ISBN-10: 0-8160-6903-4 (v. 8 : hc : alk. paper)
   ISBN-13: 978-0-8160-6904-0 (v. 9 : hc : alk. paper)
   ISBN-10: 0-8160-6904-2 (v. 9 : hc : alk. paper)
   ISBN-13: 978-0-8160-6905-7 (v. 10 : hc : alk. paper)
   ISBN-10: 0-8160-6905-0 (v. 10 : hc : alk. paper)
   ISBN-13: 978-0-8160-6906-4 (v. 11 : hc : alk. paper)
   ISBN-10: 0-8160-6906-9 (v. 11 : hc : alk. paper)
   1. Vocational guidance—United States. 2. Occupations—United States. 3. Professions—United States.
   HF5382.5.U5T677 2007
   331.7020973—dc22

                                                                          2006028638

Ferguson books are available at special discounts when purchased in bulk quantities for businesses, associations, institutions, or sales promotions. Please call our Special Sales Department in New York at (212) 967-8800 or (800) 322-8755.

You can find Ferguson on the World Wide Web at http://www.fergpubco.com

Produced by Print Matters, Inc.
Text design by A Good Thing, Inc.
Cover design by Salvatore Luongo

Printed in the United States of America

Sheridan PMI 10 9 8 7 6 5 4 3 2 1

This book is printed on acid-free paper.

Contents

How to Use This Book

This book, part of the *Top Careers in Two Years* series, highlights in-demand careers for readers considering a two-year degree program—either straight out of high school or after working a job that does not require advanced education. The focus throughout is on the fastest-growing jobs with the best potential for advancement in the field. Readers learn about future prospects while discovering jobs they may never have heard of.

An associate's degree can be a powerful tool in launching a career. This book tells you how to use it to your advantage, explore job opportunities, and find local degree programs that meet your needs.

Each chapter provides the essential information needed to find not just a job but a career that fits your particular skills and interests. All chapters include the following features:

- "Vital Statistics" provides crucial information at a glance, such as salary range, employment prospects, education or training needed, and work environment.

- Discussion of salary and wages notes hourly versus salaried situations as well as potential benefits. Salary ranges take into account regional differences across the United States.

- "Keys to Success" is a checklist of personal skills and interests needed to thrive in the career.

- "A Typical Day at Work" describes what to expect at a typical day on the job.

- "Two-Year Training" lays out the value of an associate's degree for that career and what you can expect to learn.

- "What to Look For in a School" provides questions to ask and factors to keep in mind when selecting a two-year program.

- "The Future" discusses prospects for the career going forward.

- "Interview with a Professional" presents firsthand information from someone working in the field.

- "Job Seeking Tips" offers suggestions on how to meet and work with people in the field, including how to get an internship or apprenticeship.

- "Career Connections" lists Web addresses of trade organizations providing more information about the career.

- "Associate's Degree Programs" provides a sampling of some of the better-known two-year schools.

- "Financial Aid" provides career-specific resources for financial aid.

- "Related Careers" lists similar related careers to consider.

In addition to a handy comprehensive index, the back of the book features two appendices providing invaluable information on job hunting and financial aid. Appendix A, Tools for Career Success, provides general tips on interviewing either for a job or two-year program, constructing a strong résumé, and gathering professional references. Appendix B, Financial Aid, introduces the process of applying for aid and includes information about potential sources of aid, who qualifies, how to prepare an application, and much more.

Acknowledgments

Matt Chagnon,
University of New Hampshire/Thompson School of Applied Science

John Charlton,
Zane State College

Jim Hall,
Northwest Arkansas Community College

Cindy Hammons,
Northwest Arkansas Community College

Lynda Hirose,
City College of San Francisco

Tracy Kruse,
Northeast Iowa Community College

George Macht,
College of DuPage

Terry Patterson,
College of Southern Idaho

Bob Peregoy,
Spokane Community College

Linda Pope,
Southwest Tennessee Community College

Carrie Powers,
Future Farmers of America

Kirsten Schaefer,
Gateway Community College

Frances Whited,
Agricultural Technical Institute/Ohio State University

Introduction

For millions of Americans, associate's degrees provide essential training needed to pursue a rewarding career path without the expense of a four-year degree. The U.S. Department of Education's National Center for Education Statistics found that by the end of 2005, more than 6.1 million students were enrolled in degree-granting two-year institutions—that's more than 40 percent of all the college students in the United States. The number of associate's degrees conferred continues to increase each year.

Why are increasing numbers of students taking the community college route? One central reason is that some of the fastest growing jobs in the country require only associate's degree training. What's more, only 23 percent of jobs in the 21st century require a four-year degree. In addition, many of the jobs that require only a two-year degree, such as electrician, machinist, and construction worker, are considered recession proof.

You'd expect associate's degree holders in general to earn more than those who hold only a high school degree, and they do: $2,000–$6,000 a year more on average. Community college graduates also face a much lower rate of unemployment than high school graduates. However, community college graduates with technical skills do well even when compared with four-year college graduates. Consider that 43 percent of four-year college graduates are underemployed, which means they may be taking jobs at fast food chains. On the other hand, there's a shortage of people with technical skills, including those trained at the two-year level.

"A four-year degree is a ticket to get in line for an oversold airplane," says Kenneth C. Gray, a professor of workforce education and development at Penn State University. For people with technical skills, however, including those trained at the two-year level, "There are more seats on the airplane than people holding tickets."

An Affordable Route

Probably the greatest advantage of community colleges is their lower cost. The latest statistics from the College Board show that the average annual tuition and fees for 2005–2006 at a four-year private college (excluding room and board) is $21,235, while the annual cost at a public two-year institution averages $2,191. And here's a little secret: Financial aid is not just for four-year students. Those attending trade, technical, vocational, two-year, and career colleges also can qualify for aid. You can find out more at the Department of Education's financial-aid pages: http://www.ed.gov/finaid/info/find/edpicks.jhtml?src=ov.

The College Board reports that grant aid averages about $2,300 per student for those attending two-year public colleges; however, schools that offer federal financing must be accredited. (Be very careful of "diploma mills." These are institutions that award useless diplomas, don't prepare their students properly for serious careers, take their student's tuition money, and leave them saddled with loans.) The U.S. Department of Education provides a list of accredited institutions at http://www.ope.ed.gov/accreditation/index.asp.

Regional and National Accrediting Agencies Recognized by the United States Department of Education

✔ Accrediting Council for Independent Colleges and Schools

✔ Distance Education and Training Council

✔ Middle States Association of Colleges and Schools

✔ New England Association of Schools and Colleges

✔ North Central Association of Colleges and Schools

✔ Northwest Association of Schools and Colleges

✔ Southern Association of Colleges and Schools

✔ Western Association of Schools and Colleges

Just as with four-year students, two-year students who want a piece of the aid pie usually must file the Free Application for Federal Student Aid (FAFSA). Lenders are increasingly helping two-year students as well. SallieMae (http://www.salliemae.com), the federal government student-loan agency, offers very specific private loans for career training, and U.S. Bank just introduced the CampUS Education Loan specifically for those attending two-year schools. You should note, however, that in order to receive federal Title IV financial aid, students have to declare a major field of study. (For more on the financial aid process, see Appendix B.)

In addition, two-year college students majoring in science- and technology-related subjects are also eligible for $750 and $1,300 grants. Since most of the careers in food, agriculture, and natural resources are science- and technology-related, this grant program is tailor made for students interested in this area. The grants are available under a new $790 million Academic Competitiveness Grant program unveiled in 2006 by Secretary of Education Margaret Spellings. An estimated 425,000 first- or second-year students are expected to receive grants during the first year of the program, which is described at http://www.ed.gov/policy/highered/guid/secletter/060502.html.

Great Reasons to Go

Cost savings is only one reason to consider a two-year program. Others include:

The diversity of programs. The variety of two-year training programs has exploded over the past 10 years. Associate's degrees are available not only in more traditional fields such as health care, accounting, and programming, but also in cutting-edge areas such as e-mail commerce, nanotechnology, the culinary arts, and computer animation. As for food, agriculture, and environmental programs, virtually any field you can think of has a two-year component, from aquaculture and water quality management to agricultural economics.

Flexibility. Community colleges are highly responsive to the real-life needs of their students. Classes are often offered at night, and there are seldom any residence requirements since most students commute to class. What's more, a growing number of programs are now taught, at least in part, via the Internet. The only drawback to this flexibility is that it takes the average community college student longer to complete an associate's degree—about three and a half years, according to one study. However, students looking for a more traditional college experience will find that at least 20 percent of two-year colleges provide housing, cafeterias, sports, clubs, and a bustling social scene.

Career-driven programs. Another unique aspect of associate's degree programs is that they tend to be very occupation oriented—far more so than four-year programs. Students spend a great deal of time getting hands-on experience. They may work on-site in a variety of settings or they may perform practical exercises in the classroom to gain real-world experience. For example, students at the Art Institute of Pittsburgh helped design a bicycle that scientists could use in Antarctica—drawing up blueprints and creating a prototype. This gives community college students the real-world experience that employers often require even for entry-level positions. What's more, many internships and apprenticeships lead directly to full-time employment.

Credit transfers. Here's an important but overlooked aspect of attending community college: Students who start with a two-year degree often continue on with their higher education—pursuing a four-year degree and transferring credits earned from their two-year program. One extensive study showed that over a six-year period, half of all community-college students earned an associate's degree, passed a certificate course, or transferred to a four-year college. Some even went on to earn a more advanced professional degree. The credits are transferable at many two-year colleges. Note, however, that credits earned at a two-year college do not automatically transfer to a four-year program. If you have even the slightest hunch that someday you may want to transfer to a four-year program, find out now about the transfer process from the two-year colleges you're considering. You may even want to double check with the four-year colleges as well.

Less competitive pressure. Another great feature about associate's degree programs is that admission is not overly competitive. Students are admitted from a wide range of academic backgrounds. What's more, the professors and educators are far more dedicated to teaching. They don't face pressure to conduct research and publish scholarly articles. They can be much more invested in helping interested students succeed. All this means that students who performed below average in high school can excel at a two-year school if they put in the time and energy.

Choosing a Career in Food, Agriculture, or Natural Resources

In this volume, you'll find a wide variety of interesting careers, all of which share certain characteristics. First, these jobs are dependent to some degree on weather, climate, and the yearly cycle of seasons. The menu of a restaurant that serves a large proportion of fresh foods, for instance, will alter somewhat in summer and winter. Farmers, whether they are cultivating alfalfa or fish, must plant and harvest according to Mother Nature's timetable if they are to succeed. Workers in the natural resources sector always factor weather changes into their jobs. Forest technicians, for instance, must be prepared to deal with tree "blow downs," which high winds cause. Wastewater treatment plant operators must be able to deal with heavy rains, which can lead to sewage backups.

Second, weather and climate determine to some degree whether many jobs in agriculture and natural resources will be performed outdoors or indoors on any given day. (By contrast, most employees in the food industry work indoors, although weather may still determine how many customers show up at a local restaurant.)

Third, a substantial minority—46 percent—of all workers in food, agriculture, forestry, and fishing are self-employed, according to the U.S. Department of Labor's Bureau of Labor Statistics. Even in the food service industry, in which most managers are salaried, "more than 40 percent are self-employed in independent restaurants and other small food service establishments."

Despite their similarities, careers in each of these sectors also have major differences. Let's take a look.

Food

Jobs in this food service category covered in this book are food service manager and dietetic technician. *Restaurant and food service managers* usually are responsible for the day-to-day operations of a restaurant or cafeteria. They work in restaurants in which anyone may walk in the door on a given day and expect to be fed any dish on the menu. The emphasis is on taste, variety, and attractive presentation. *Dietetic technicians*, on the other hand, work primarily in institutions such as hospitals, senior citizen centers, and nursing homes, in which the number of diners is more predictable and the décor may tend toward institutional green. Here the menu is more limited and the primary considerations are the nutritional needs of the clients, who may have medical problems that require special diets.

Food service managers and dietetic technicians share more characteristics than you might think. Both are responsible for planning menus, analyzing recipes, ordering food, determining and controlling food costs, preparing meals, supervising food production and service, developing job descriptions, and keeping track of work schedules. To carry out these tasks, both jobs require organizational abilities, written and oral communication skills, and experience in establishing and maintaining interpersonal relationships, making decisions, and solving problems. In both jobs, employees work under time pressure and as part of a team. To be a good food service manager or dietetic technician, it also helps to have an entrepreneurial streak, or at least the touch of a salesperson, because in both jobs you're looking for a way to make your menus more attractive, even if the reasons for doing it are different. The food service manager is usually trying to raise his or her profit margin by getting more people in the door. Dietetic technicians, on the other hand, must use their persuasive powers to get their clients to eat nutritionally necessary foods to which they may not be accustomed.

Agriculture

Jobs in this category that are covered in this volume include horticulture technician, landscaping supervisor, animal husbandry manager, dairy farm manager, and agribusiness manager. (The U.S. Department of Labor also includes forestry and fishing in the same general category as agriculture, while we have grouped them with Natural Resources—see below.) *Horticulture technicians* know how to grow, maintain, and market ornamental plants. *Landscaping supervisors* specialize in the planning, cultivation, and maintenance of lawns and grounds for individuals, businesses, and sports facilities. *Animal husbandry managers* run farms that raise livestock, usually cows, poultry, or swine. *Dairy farm managers* run dairy farms that produce milk and milk products. *Agribusiness managers* produce, sell, and distribute fertilizer, feed, machinery, and other products needed by farmers.

With over 2 million workers, agriculture is one of the largest industries in the United States. Of these workers, salaried employees outnumber the self-employed by 8 percent. While relatively small family farms account for almost 90 percent of the total number of farms, the remaining 10 percent produce 75 percent of the nation's agricultural output. Farms that produce crops have jobs that are more seasonal, involving planting, growing, and harvesting. Farms that raise animals, by contrast, have jobs that must be done year round, such as milking, feeding, exercising, and assisting at births. While much of the work on both types of farms is highly mechanized, planting and harvesting some crops still require large numbers of people, and any manager of animal husbandry will tell you how much he or she depends on others, if only for advice.

Whether they raise crops or animals, or deal with the products needed to raise these crops and animals, all who work in agriculture obviously must know a great deal about living things—which animals to breed, the best conditions under which crops and animals grow, and what to do when they fail to thrive. A love of the outdoors is also important since the vast majority of the work takes place there in all kinds of weather. The ability to work well with others also is crucial, since agricultural production is a task that often involves a group of people working as a team. Since agriculture is a business, knowledge of business skills, such as accounting, economics, and mathematics is also essential. Physical stamina is a consideration as well, since most people who work in agriculture put in a long day and are often on their feet.

Natural Resources

Jobs in this category covered in this book include wildlife technician, water and wastewater treatment plant operator, and forest technician. *Wildlife technicians* provide support and services to scientists who work in wildlife management and animal biology. *Water or wastewater treatment plant operators* are responsible for ensuring that the water we drink and the sewage we dispose of are treated so that they are safe for us and the environment. *Forest technicians* do the same thing for scientists who work in forest management.

Due to weather changes among spring, summer, fall, and winter, many jobs in this broad sector are either seasonal, or the work is divided between warm-weather field work, such as gathering of data, and cold-weather projects, such as planning and analysis of data. The exception to this seasonal pattern is water treatment plant operators, whose plants operate 24 hours a day all year round. These operators work both indoors and outdoors no matter what the season. In all natural resource–related jobs, as in agricultural jobs, if you work outdoors you can expect to find yourself occasionally working under extreme weather conditions—it's an aspect of the job that comes with the territory.

Despite the variety of natural resource–related jobs, all the jobs described in this section share some similar, if not identical, tasks. In all four jobs, you'll find yourself collecting data or samples, whether it's counting wildlife, weighing young fish, measuring trees, or taking water samples. All four jobs also involve maintaining equipment, including repairing bird traps, cleaning fish ponds, checking the gas mixture in a chain saw, or fixing a water pump. In all these jobs you'll also use computers to map and compile data, maintain study records, and keep track of sales figures. Depending on the job and your level of experience, eventually you may find yourself either training other workers or representing your agency or organization with the public.

What's Best for You?

How can you decide which of the three fields (or any of the other fields covered in this series, for that matter) is best for you? In which job within a given field are you most likely to succeed? To begin to find out, you might make a list of the most enjoyable experiences you have ever had, whether they took place on the job, in school, or elsewhere. The experience might have been reading a book that gave you a new appreciation of animals, or finding a hobby such as stamp collecting that led you to discover the world of geography. When you have a list of 10 or 20 such experiences, list what it was about each experience that made it so exciting and worthwhile. For example, what was it about animals that made them intriguing? Was it their peculiar physical traits? Their need for care? What was it about foreign countries that grabbed your attention? Was it the unfamiliar customs of their inhabitants? Or the similarities that lurked just beneath the superficial differences?

Once you have gone through each experience and decided what made it attractive, sift through all the factors on your list and look for similarities. For example, did you see a similarity between your attraction to the peculiar traits of animals and the odd customs of foreigners? That clue could mean that a job featuring an exotic or offbeat setting or unusual coworkers may be attractive to you. Once you have found a group of such common factors, you can use these as another checklist when examining potential jobs in this book. A job that seems likely to meet the criteria on your checklist is one that you will want to look at seriously.

Explore the careers in food, agriculture, and natural resources using the information and techniques described in this book. Your goal is to select a job that will fully engage your interests, talents, skills, and abilities and bring you both financial and rewards and job satisfaction. Good luck on your journey!

Horticulture Technician

Vital Statistics

Salary: The average annual salary for a horticulture technician is $28,579, according to 2006 data from the U.S. Bureau of Labor Statistics. However, wages vary widely by region and season.

Employment: Opportunities for horticulture technicians, ground maintenance workers, and landscapers are better than average because of high job turnover and increasing demand for landscaping.

Education: A two-year horticulture degree or certificate is very helpful, although not essential.

Work Environment: Horticulture technicians work in garden centers, nurseries, parks, or laboratories. They are outside a great deal in varying weather.

When you look at the lush grounds and plantings that bring so much beauty to parks, parkways, and public and private gardens, you might imagine that they just grow there naturally. Yet these "passages of scenery," as the great landscape architect Frederick L. Olmsted, described them, take countless hours of planning, creation, and maintenance by horticulturalists. These skilled individuals specialize in the cultivation and maintenance of plants.

Horticulture technicians have the knowledge and resourcefulness to create the conditions for countless varieties of plants to thrive. Whether they're tending delicate lavender bushes or hardy shrub roses, horticulture technicians germinate the seeds, nurture the seedlings in a greenhouse, transplant them to an outside location where they'll thrive, and arrange them as part of a garden display. Some technicians also conduct experiments to find the best growing techniques for that particular species. Depending on the season, horticulture technicians may change their job location. During the warmer months, they may work outside on maintenance crews; during the winter, they may work indoors in nurseries or botanical gardens.

Some horticulture technicians specialize in other ways as well. Some run nurseries or grow plants for landscaping companies. Some consult or advise landscape architects or research specific plant diseases. Others may work at rehabilitation centers using plants to help those with emotional or physical disabilities to recover or adjust to their special needs. By helping a garden to grow or a plant to thrive, disabled people may gain increased confidence in managing their disability.

As horticulture technicians gain experience, they may advance to supervisory positions or start their own nurseries, landscape maintenance businesses, or import-export companies. Also they may work for state or local governments, public park and recreation departments, or large companies with horticultural needs.

Horticulture technicians also can open doors for themselves by going back to school. There they can retrain or upgrade their skills to become arborists, landscape architects, or land-use planners. They also can advance their education and career prospects while they're on the job by working toward advanced certificates in their field. For instance, the CHT (certified horticulture technician) certificate confirms that the applicant has worked in the industry for over 2,000 hours, half of which may come from education in a postsecondary school diploma program. Applicants also must pass a series of written and practical evaluations in any one of four areas: landscape installation, landscape maintenance, retail garden center, and interiorscape. Whatever they do, they'll develop the technical and aesthetic skills to turn land into landscapes. In doing their jobs, they'll have the satisfaction of knowing that they nurture living plants that enrich everyone's lives.

On the Job

It takes a grab bag of skills and talents to produce a beautiful display of plants. To bring a seed from germination to full flower, and then maintain it for its natural life, a horticulture technician does plenty of planting, watering, fertilizing, and pruning, of course. It's physically demanding work. Just imagine hauling around large bags of fertilizer, bending over to transplant seedlings, regularly pruning and weeding, and working outside in all kinds of weather. You'll also need to be mentally alert and physically adept to operate machinery such as power clippers, edgers, and mowers. Horticulturalists work on a schedule that is determined largely by nature's timetables, not ours. Like farmers, occasionally they must put in long hours at a stretch so the plants they work with have the greatest chance to survive and thrive.

> **"Plants provide us with food, shelter, medicines, energy sources, clothing, and the very air we breathe. They temper the climate and help hold the planet intact . . . and they're beautiful!"**
> —Linda Gombert, display garden horticulturist

In addition to physical labor, horticulture technicians rely on their reading skills. They must be able to decipher warning labels on fungicides and pesticides as well as the finer points of catalogue entries, including the Latin names of plants. Math also comes in handy. They use it, for instance, when they're comparing data from soil samples to determine the effect of different fertilizers, and when they're figuring out how much water to mix with an herbicide to create the right concentrate to cover a particular property.

Horticulture technicians need strong communication skills to take instructions and clarify specific tasks. They must be able to advise customers on their purchases and talk to suppliers about orders and delivery schedules. In their free time, horticulture technicians also are expected to keep up with changing trends in gardening by reading catalogues and trade publications.

All these needs and tasks add up to a job that can be mentally and physically challenging. The rewards are satisfied customers and the chance to make the world a more beautiful place.

Keys to Success

To be a successful horticulture technician, you should have (a) strong

- ☞ passion for plants and gardening
- ☞ curiosity about the science of plants
- ☞ stamina
- ☞ communication skills
- ☞ sense of aesthetics
- ☞ interest in improving the environment
- ☞ conscientiousness and responsibility

Do You Have What It Takes?

Do you like to grow beautiful living things without minding whether you get your hands dirty doing it? Would you enjoy using your creativity to arrange plantings in a pleasing manner? Do you have the stamina to work outdoors when necessary in all sorts of weather tending to your plants? Is your idea of relaxation kicking back with plant catalogues? If you've always liked being around flowers, trees, and ornamental shrubs, then you may enjoy being a horticulture technician. One warning, however: Those who are allergic to certain plants, pollens, or agricultural chemicals or pesticides may have difficulty working in this occupation.

A Typical Day at Work

How horticulture technicians spend their day depends partly on where they work. For instance, if you work for a state or local government, public garden, or large landscaping company, you might begin your day in the spring and summer with a group meeting. There you would receive your daily tasks. The rest of the day you might maintain the plantings at the parks and recreation area, and you might well work overtime. During the colder months, you would spend most of your time indoors restocking inventories of materials and equipment and maintaining machinery.

If you work for a private business, such as a retail garden center, nursery, or botanical and horticultural garden, you generally would keep more regular hours and spend more time selling plants and supplies to retail customers. Still, you might need to put in extra hours when a large order needs to be filled quickly.

Whether you work for a public or private organization, however, you would probably spend most of your time digging, fertilizing, and watering the plants for which you are responsible. The work might take place indoors in a climate-controlled nursery, or outside. You also would spend part of the typical day consulting with coworkers, monitoring plants, and keeping records.

How to Break In

Summer jobs, part-time work, or even volunteering often can lead to a career in this field. Today there are more than 1.1 million workers in the general field of landscaping and groundskeeping. With a high turnover rate, and few job entry requirements, you will always find openings available if you are interested in ornamental plants and willing to work hard. High school students who have taken biology, botany, and other courses in math and science have an advantage over the competition, as would members of organizations such as Future Farmers of America (FFA). Once you have some experience, you can apply to schools for a certificate or two-year program and continue to do seasonal or part-time work, often for credit as part of your degree.

Two-Year Training

Scores of community colleges and technical schools offer two-year associate's degree programs for horticulture technicians. This degree is the key to working as a horticulturalist in a variety of settings. Some programs combine horticulture and landscape management, while others separate them (see Chapter 2 for programs that specialize in training landscapers and groundskeepers).

Horticulture technicians take courses on growing and caring for ornamental plants, shrubs, and trees; installation of landscape materials; nursery crop production; garden center sales; and operation of landscape and nursery equipment. Plant-specific courses include plant identification, propagation, and development; pruning; soils and fertilizers; and landscape design. Students also take classes in written communication and speech, mathematics, social sciences, humanities, and computer applications.

Horticulture degree programs combine classroom and lab work with internships, so students get hands-on experience. This may take place in a garden center, landscaping company, public parks department, arboretum, golf course, or estate. At the end of a two-year program in horticultural science, the graduating horticulture technician is prepared for any of several occupations, including nursery and garden center manager and associate, nursery producer, greenhouse grower, organic food producer, supply and equipment salesperson, landscape designer, installation and maintenance worker, or parks department worker.

Horticulture technicians who wish to further their education after graduating may pursue the CHT certificate described above.

What to Look For in a School

When considering a two-year school, be sure to ask these questions:

☞ Will the school teach me the basic skills in horticultural science?

☞ Will I learn additional skills in agricultural and small business management, communications, and computer applications?

☞ Will the school help me obtain internships?

☞ What kinds of jobs do the school's graduates get, and what is the school's job-placement rate?

☞ Does the school offer courses in those aspects of horticulture that interest me?

☞ What are the professors' credentials and experience? Have they worked in the horticultural industry? Are they available outside the classroom and by e-mail?

☞ What are the laboratory, greenhouse, and classroom facilities like? Is the equipment up-to-date?

Did You Know?

Luther Burbank (1849–1926), the most famous horticulturalist born in the United States, developed more than 800 new plant varieties during his lifetime.

Interview with a Professional:
Q&A
Ron Worgul
Co-manager, Rosedale Nurseries, Hawthorne, New York

Q: *How did you get started?*

A: I've always loved plants and insects, so I decided to apply to colleges with a landscape program. As the next year wore on, I found myself not enjoying the mechanical drawing aspect as much as the outdoor aspects—installing, pruning, and working in the greenhouses. So I changed my major to nursery management. I had started working in a sales position here part-time while in school. Once I graduated, I joined full time.

Q: *What's a typical day like?*

A: In spring I'll start at about 7 a.m. and go until about 6 p.m. The morning starts with informing the staff of what shipments may be coming in and coordinating with the other managers to get the unloading completed. At the same time, I'll answer questions from the staff, the landscape office, and customers. Throughout the day, I also write up customer's delivery orders. Once deliveries are unloaded, we make sure everything is priced properly and displayed to make the product appealing. Each morning I also scout for potential plants to bring up to the store. When we are out of items such as soils, mulches, fertilizers, and chemicals, I reorder them. I also assist customers and direct the sales staff on who would be most appropriate with certain customers.

Q: *What's your advice for those starting a career?*

A: First, it's very important for anyone getting into the horticultural industry to learn about plants! You can't advise a consumer about what works in what location without understanding where plants like to grow.

Q: *What's the best part of being a horticulture technician?*

A: I love to walk through my gardens as they are growing through the spring, summer, and fall. By experimenting with plants in various locations in my gardens, I'm able to answer a lot of different questions customers may have. Of course, the end result is a beautiful garden.

The Future

The future is indeed rosy for the horticultural industry, with employment expected to increase about 20 percent over the next five to 10 years. In addition, opportunities for advancement should also increase. Currently there are about 61,000 first-line supervisory employees in the grouping that includes horticulture technicians. This number should grow by about 14,000 additional employees by 2014.

The reasons for all of this growth are literally everywhere. Both housing and commercial construction have been increasing, and well-kept gardens, lawns, and grounds boost the value of a property. In addition, more two-earner households and a boom in outdoor entertaining have created an increasing demand for horticulture technicians to take care of people's lawns and gardens. Finally, as the population ages, homeowners will require outside help to maintain their yards.

Job Seeking Tips

✔ Use family and friends to find contacts in the field and interview these contacts for information and job leads.

✔ Seek job experience in different areas such as grounds maintenance and nursery work.

✔ Decide what aspect of horticulture you're interested in and seek further relevant experience.

✔ Talk to the career placement office.

✔ Be proactive and persistent in following up job leads.

Career Connections

For further information, contact the following organizations.

The **American Horticultural Society** is oriented toward practicing gardeners. The AHS maintains a Web site with excellent links and resources.   http://www.ahs.org

The **American Horticultural Therapy Association** holds conferences, publishes a journal, and acts as a data clearinghouse. http://www.ahta.org

The **American Society for Horticultural Science** promotes horticulture research and education. Its Web site features career profiles and job listings.   http://www.ashs.org

The **California Occupational Guides** are designed for the California job market. These pages provide valuable information about horticultural careers.   http://www.labormarketinfo.edd.ca.gov

Future Farmers of America   http://www.ffa.org

The **Professional Landcare Network (PLANET)** runs an accreditation program, awards scholarships, and provides other services for its members and the public.   http://www.landcarenetwork.org

Associate's Degree Programs

Here are just a few schools that offer quality horticulture technician programs:

Clackamas Community College, Oregon City, Oregon

Illinois Central College, East Peoria, Illinois

Miami Dade College, Miami, Florida

Naugatuck Valley Community College, Waterbury, Connecticut

Pennsylvania College of Technology, Williamsport, Pennsylvania

Financial Aid

Here are a few horticulture-related scholarships. Students should also check state-level nursery and agricultural organizations for scholarship possibilities. For more on financial aid for two-year students, turn to Appendix B.

The **ALCA Educational Foundation (AEF)**, founded to award scholarships and fund educational activities for the landscape industry, has raised over $1 million from donors within the landscape industry. Scholarship applicants and recipients must be enrolled at a school that is accredited by the Professional Landcare Network (PLANET), has a PLANET student chapter membership, or that participates in PLANET career days. http://www.landcarenetwork.org

The **National Future Farmers of America (FFA) Scholarship Program** awards over $2 million in scholarships each year to FFA members with a wide variety of career plans. http://www.ffa.org

Related Careers

Landscape architect, biological scientist, county cooperative extension agent, agricultural inspector, agricultural or nursery manager, farmer, rancher, forester, arborist, and sales representative.

Landscaping Supervisor

Vital Statistics

Salary: The average salary for a landscaping supervisor or grounds manager is about $30,922 a year, according to 2006 data from the U.S. Bureau of Labor Statistics.

Employment: The number of jobs for grounds managers and landscaping supervisors will increase faster than the average over the next five years.

Education: Grounds managers and landscape supervisors usually require education beyond high school and job experiences with increasing responsibilities. An associate of applied science (A.A.S) degree also demonstrates knowledge necessary to pass state certification and licensing tests.

Work Environment: Landscaping supervisors work indoors planning and tracking construction projects. Sometimes they work outdoors installing and maintaining projects in settings ranging from golf courses to industrial parks.

Why do so many people seek out parks, outdoor athletic facilities, and other oases of greenery? Probably because we find the open space, running water, decorative plantings, and relative quiet restful and recreational. When we leave such areas, we feel relaxed and revived.

Landscaping supervisors and grounds managers create and maintain these peaceful, useful, and beautiful environments. As some open lands turn into housing developments and malls, these little oases become ever more important in our lives. This means that the role of the landscaping or grounds manager will be in even greater demand.

The jobs of landscaping manager and grounds manager are similar and often overlap. The difference is that landscapers are generally more involved in the actual construction and installation of landscaped areas. They build walkways with a particular slope or slant in order to promote better drainage. They install lighting or sprinkler systems as well as perform the usual planting and caring for plants, trees, shrubs, and lawns. Grounds managers, on the other hand, are usually more involved in the maintenance of landscaped areas. They repair and clear snow from those walkways, adjust sprinkler systems to save water, monitor natural turf to make sure it is draining properly, and clean artificial turf on athletic fields, replacing it when necessary.

In carrying out and supervising these tasks, landscape and grounds managers must be familiar with a variety of tools, including shovels, rakes, saws, axes, and trimmers. They use machines including power lawnmowers, chain saws, snowblowers, electric clippers, sod cutters, and sometimes tractors. In addition, landscape and grounds managers must understand a lot about pesticides, herbicides, fungicides, and insecticides and must be able to apply them properly (unless a subcontractor is hired). Also, they supervise their crews.

Other landscaping specialties include tree trimmers and tree pruners, who are supervised by arborists. Arborists are specialists in the characteristics and care of individual trees. They can tell you which trees are most likely to thrive in a particular location.

Grounds maintenance is a booming field today with about 1.5 million jobs. Of these, about 184,000 are as supervisors of landscaping, lawn service, or groundskeeping workers. Since demand for their services is increasing, the opportunities for advancement in this field are very good. In addition to an associate's degree or the equivalent in educational credits, advancement generally requires one or more advanced certificates, such as Certified Landscape Professional, Certified Landscape Technician, Certified Turfgrass Professional, and Certified Ornamental Landscape Professional.

On the Job

Managers of landscaping and grounds maintenance workers must be familiar with all the tasks assigned to those who work under them—everything from installing irrigation systems to operating heavy machinery. That's because one of their jobs is to train these workers. In addition, landscaping and grounds managers prepare cost estimates for the work projects they supervise. They plan the work schedules for their crews, check that the work is being performed satisfactorily, keep records of what is accomplished, and tally how long their workers are on the job each day. If the work is not performed correctly, or if the details of the project change, then the manager must suggest changes and see that they are carried out. If additional crew members are needed to complete a project on time, landscape and grounds supervisors themselves will usually pitch in to help.

Landscape and grounds managers therefore require leadership skills and the ability to foster a cooperative team spirit. Communication skills are crucial. Command of a foreign language (or the ability to learn one) is a definite plus, since grounds maintenance workers may be recent immigrants.

Landscapers and grounds manager always need to keep their clients in mind. So they must use their communications skills to translate their client's vision into a reality as well as to communicate their own suggestions. They must be dependable, flexible, responsible, and be able to coordinate a variety of activities.

🔑 Keys to Success

To be a successful landscaper, you should have (a) strong

- ⚷ motivational and decision-making skills
- ⚷ sense of enterprise
- ⚷ knowledge of landscaping tools and machinery
- ⚷ physical fitness
- ⚷ love of working outdoors
- ⚷ knowledge of plants

A Typical Day at Work

The day begins early for most landscape and grounds managers, especially during the growing seasons. That's because the cool early mornings are the most comfortable outdoor hours. First, landscaping managers review the day's assigned jobs, and make sure the crew is at their posts and has the tools and machinery they need. If deliveries of work materials are scheduled, the manager checks the timing of the drop-offs and whether everything ordered is in the shipment. As the day goes on, the manager may travel among different work sites to monitor progress, assist workers where needed, assess any problems that come up, and note any current or future needs. For example, if a mowing machine has broken a blade, the manager makes sure that a replacement machine is available and that a new blade is ordered.

After supervising workers, landscaping and grounds managers may return to their office. Here they review contracts for upcoming projects to make sure the contracts specify the correct service, machine, and workforce requirements for the job. They may prepare cost estimates for prospective customers and address customers' questions and complaints (if there are any). Toward the end of their day, managers assess the progress on their current projects and review the next day's work schedule.

Do You Have What It Takes?

Do you like to make green things grow? Would you like to plan and execute a lawn and gardening project? Do you enjoy wielding a shovel or a rake or supervising those who do? These are some of the tasks of a landscaping manager or grounds manager. Students interested in landscaping and grounds management should enjoy being outside and cultivating the natural environment so that it looks its best. If you get a feeling of satisfaction after mowing a shaggy lawn or trimming a ragged hedge, this may a career in which you can find fulfillment.

How to Break In

While in high school, students interested in landscaping or groundskeeping careers should learn everything they can about the science of plants and how to care for them. In addition to taking classes in biology and botany, they should also acquire skills and experience in machinery repair and get summer or part-time jobs in gardening and lawn maintenance.

Your associate's degree in landscape management or grounds maintenance will distinguish you from the majority of workers in this field. With any luck, a student internship will pave the way for a full-time position. So will taking the following steps: getting recommendations from your teachers; job references; a portfolio of projects you've worked on; and a network of contacts from fellow students, faculty, and horticulture club members.

Then drop off your résumé at the local parks or highway department, athletic facilities, or corporate or university campuses, and follow up regularly.

> **"This is a pretty neat industry because you can be outdoors in the middle of Mother Nature. There is an inner peace that comes with that, and I always feel I am contributing to the environment."**
> —Mark Henning, owner, landscape services company

Two-Year Training

There is no shortage of two-year degree programs in landscaping and grounds management. One popular college guide lists over three dozen institutions that offer an A.A.S degree in this area. As noted in Chapter 1, some programs combine offerings in horticultural science and landscape management, while others allow students to specialize to varying degrees in one area or the other. Some graduates with a strong background in both horticulture and landscaping may be more likely to find themselves working in nurseries, greenhouses, theme parks, and arboretums. Graduates with a focus on landscape management, however, will find their way to positions with property management and real-estate development firms, lawn and garden equipment and supply stores, amusement and recreation facilities, corporate headquarters, and local governments

The best two-year landscape management programs combine classroom, laboratory, and practical educational experiences. These experiences usually take the form of internships with local businesses. A typical two-year program will include a total of 60 or more credits in landscape-specific courses such as landscape design, planning, construction, maintenance, and business operations; and turf management operations, plant pathology, pest management, irrigation and drainage, and soil technology. More basic courses will include botany, entomology, communications, computer applications, and business mathematics.

What to Look For in a School

When looking for a two-year school, be sure to ask questions like these:

☞ Will the school teach me the basic skills in landscape or grounds management?

☞ Will I learn additional skills in landscape design, pest management, computer technology, and aboriculture?

☞ Will the school help me obtain internships?

☞ Does the school offer enough variety in courses that I can find an area that interests me?

☞ What are the professors' credentials and experience? Have they worked in the landscape industry? Are they available outside the classroom and by e-mail?

☞ What are the physical facilities like? Are the classroom materials and training equipment up to date?

The Future

Business is booming in the landscaping and grounds-maintenance industry. Housing and commercial real estate markets are aiming to increase the value of properties by adding new lawns and grounds or improving existing ones. This means more managers will be required to supervise the increasing number of workers needed to keep up these properties. The rise in demand also should lead to a growing number of entrepreneurial opportunities for landscaping contractors. In addition, as the population ages, homeowners will turn to landscaping companies.

Did You Know?

Frederick Law Olmsted (1822–1903) created the field of landscape architecture. He and his firm designed signature parks—such as New York's Central Park—in over a dozen U.S. and Canadian cities. His work includes the park systems of Seattle, Boston, and Louisville.

Interview with a Professional:
Q&A

Teresa Riddle

Head landscaper, Spokane Country Club,
Spokane, Washington

Q: *How did you get started?*

A: All my life I have been a gardener. It's my passion. I thought I'd really like to be a landscape consultant, but I wanted more education. I started with the horticulture department at Spokane Community College, and I am so thankful that I took that step. I thought I knew a lot about landscapes and plants, but I learned so much more. I also took part in the horticulture clubs and competitions. All of that helped me with the interview process, networking, business, and self-esteem.

Q: *What's a typical day like?*

A: Each season brings on new tasks. During peak season, there are daily tasks like watering, mowing, deadheading (picking dead blossoms from plants), and general cleanup. The rest of the day will vary, though it may include plant health care, planting or planning gardens, teaching classes, or record keeping.

Q: *What is your advice for those starting out in this career?*

A: Get an education in your area of interest, even if you have been working in that field. If your career goal is landscape design, work during different seasons on an installation crew, a pruning crew, a nursery crew, and an irrigation crew. The more you do, the better understanding you will have of all the components that go into a great design.

Q: *What is the best part of being a landscaper?*

A: It's getting to work outside with nature and beauty all around every single day. There's just something about getting your hands in the soil, experiencing the scent of the elements, and being a part of the process of making things beautiful for others that is very fulfilling to me.

Job Seeking Tips

✔ Take courses in biology, chemistry, computer applications, business, and math.

✔ Do a computer search of landscape/grounds manager and find out everything you can about the field.

✔ Decide what aspects of the field you are interested in and seek relevant experience.

✔ Talk to the career placement office at school about career paths.

Career Connections

For further information, contact state landscape and grounds management associations, landscape contractor organizations, state and local government park departments, plus these national organizations:

The **Professional Grounds Management Society** offers a Certified Grounds Manager (CGM) certificate to those with a combination of eight years of education and experience beyond high school, and who pass an examination. http://www.pgms.org

The **Professional Landcare Network (PLANET)** awards scholarships and provides other services for its members and the public. http://www.landcarenetwork.org

The **Tree Care Industry Association** provides career and certification information. http://www.TreeCareIndustry.org

Associate's Degree Programs

Here are a few schools offering quality landscape management and grounds management programs:

County College of Morris, Randolph, New Jersey

Cuyahoga Community College, Cleveland, Ohio

Richland College, Dallas, Texas

Southwest Tennessee Community College, Memphis, Tennessee

Spokane Community College, Spokane, Washington

Springfield Technical Community College, Springfield, Massachusetts

Financial Aid

Here are a few landscape-related scholarships. In addition to federal, state, and specific college-related aid, students should check state-level nursery and landscape industry organizations for scholarship possibilities. For more on financial aid for two-year students, turn to Appendix B.

The **ALCA Educational Foundation (AEF)**, awards scholarships and funds educational activities for the landscape industry. Scholarship applicants and recipients must be enrolled at a school that is accredited by the Professional Landcare Network (PLANET), has a PLANET Student Chapter membership, or that participates in PLANET Career Days. http://www.landcarenetwork.org

The **National Future Farmers of America (FFA) Scholarship Program** awards over $2 million each year in scholarships to FFA members with a wide variety of postsecondary career plans.   http://www.ffa.org

The **Professional Grounds Management Society** offers the Anne Seaman Memorial Scholarship to those interested in pursuing higher education in grounds management.   http://www.pgms.org

Related Careers

Landscape architect, agricultural manager, retail sales manager, landscape contractor, irrigation specialist, arborist, and biological scientist.

Food Service Manager

Vital statistics

Salary: Salaries range by the type of eatery from $36,290 (school cafeterias) to $43,660 (hotels and motels). The median yearly salary of a salaried food service manager is $39,600, according to 2006 data from the U.S. Bureau of Labor Statistics.

Employment: Food service management jobs are growing as the population increases. Opportunities exist in restaurants as well as educational institutions and senior centers.

Education: A two-year degree in food service management or culinary arts. Restaurant experience is highly desirable.

Work Environment: Restaurant and institutional kitchens and dining rooms of various sizes.

When most people think of dining out, they probably picture a typical neighborhood family restaurant or more upscale bistro. If they're students, they may think of a fast-food chain. But the world of dining is far larger than this. Many corporations and businesses have cafeterias, as do theme and sports parks. Meanwhile, airports, hotels, convention centers, and cruise ships all maintain restaurants. Hospitals and nursing homes must feed their clients; prisons and jails must feed their inmates. Even some day care centers provide lunch. In short, it's hard to think of a place outside the home where people routinely gather for long periods where food is not served.

It's no wonder that the food service industry includes an estimated 371,000 jobs. About 60 percent of these are salaried, usually in full-service restaurants or fast-food restaurants and cafeterias. The remaining 40 percent of food service workers are self-employed, generally in independent restaurants and other small eateries. Within this industry, the title of the employee who actually acts as the manager may vary. Often, so do the job duties. For instance, in most full-service restaurants and institutional food-service facilities, the food service manager (sometimes called the assistant manager) oversees service in the dining room, while the executive chef is in charge of all food preparation activities. This may include kitchen operations, menu planning, and quality assurance. However, in limited-service eateries, such as some corporate cafeterias, the food service manager carries out the duties of the executive chef, supervising the food preparation operations. In smaller restaurants, the distinctions between formal titles are blurred even further, as one person may do the work of more than one food service position. The food service manager may also be the cashier and receptionist, while the executive chef may also be the general manager or even an owner.

If the variety of eating establishments makes it tough to decide which type you might prefer, it helps to consider the variety of working conditions. For instance, if you'd prefer a 9 to 5 job, a limited-service operation would tend to have more regular hours. Full-service establishments, on the other hand, while they may be open fewer days of the week, also tend to be open much longer hours.

Many food service managers are trained on the job. They start out in entry-level positions, such as servers, and work their way up. Others, including executive chefs, usually receive formal training in community and junior colleges, technical institutes, and culinary institutes. Training is not only a career-boosting move, but is also increasingly an essential step to becoming a food service manager or executive chef at many upscale restaurants.

On the Job

Being a food service manager, executive chef, or other restaurant manager requires the ability to juggle tasks, organize one's time efficiently, communicate clearly, and deal with problems quickly in an often high-pressure environment. Food that is listed on the menu is expected to be available. This means the food service manager or executive chef must order food items and supplies, often in huge quantities, depending on where he or she works. In addition, it's necessary to inspect orders to make sure that everything meets the restaurant's standards. Food needs to be prepared properly also, so the food service manager or executive chef oversees the work of the kitchen staff, offering advice when necessary. Food needs to be served when it is ready—not 15 minutes later—and customer orders need to be processed quickly. So the food service manager must hire enough servers and assign their workloads so that no one server is overloaded.

> **"Always be prepared to put yourself forward, stay later, go the extra mile. It will make those in management more willing to invest time, money, training, and attention to your success."**
> —Maria Zefo, catering sales/operations manager

For most people, eating food is one of life's most pleasurable experiences, and this should include eating away from home. The food service manager aims to keep customers or clients happy by seeing that they are served tasty food in a timely manner and by resolving their complaints in order not to lose any future business. The food service manager must also keep his employees motivated in part by listening to and solving their work-related difficulties. These activities require energy and resourcefulness as the food service manager moves from task to task while keeping a watchful eye on the whole food service operation.

Sanitation, safety, and security concerns also require that the food service manager anticipate potential problems and be prepared with solutions. Is the water in the dishwasher hot enough? Are fire extinguishers properly positioned in the kitchen? Are the day's receipts safely under lock and key? Dealing with these and countless other concerns are all part of the food service manager's daily responsibilities.

Keys to Success

To be a successful food service manager, you should have (a) strong
- work habits, punctuality, and attention to detail
- ability to provide excellent customer service
- ability to work well under pressure
- self-motivation and ability to motivate others
- communication skills
- basic business skills
- understanding of food production

Do You Have What It Takes?

Students interested in the food service business should have a passion for food as well as a knack for producing meals in an organized and efficient manner. They should enjoy managing a business also. If you get satisfaction from satisfying someone with a good meal, if you have solid organizational skills and are good at motivating others, this may be a great career for you. The growing number of eating establishments as well as the high demand for food service managers make this business highly attractive for those with talent and ambition.

How to Break In

In high school, future food service managers can gain valuable experience working in restaurants or cafeterias and by taking classes in nutrition and related subjects as well as any business courses offered. Later, in a two-year program, they can select appropriate internship opportunities. These not only provide valuable hands-on experience, but may lead directly to a job following graduation. In addition, most restaurant chains and food service management companies have training programs that typically last six to twelve months, after which trainees become assistant food service managers.

As a student, also consider the opportunities available through student memberships in a professional organization like the American Hotel and Lodging Association (http://www.ahla.com) or the National Restaurant Association (http://www.restaurant.org). Both associations offer informative e-mail news services and networking opportunities. Another possibility is to look for training, part-time work, or an internship through the school's food-service program. In addition, use every food-related job to observe how successful managers operate.

Job hunters in this field should highlight their initiative and leadership skills. Also, they should be able to demonstrate that they have good memories for details and are efficient problem-solvers. A well-groomed appearance is essential because managers deal directly with the public.

A Typical Day at Work

No matter what type of establishment the food service manager works for, he or she is usually the first to arrive in the morning and the last to leave at night. At some facilities and restaurants, the manager may arrive as early as 5 a.m. He or she is responsible for tasks ranging from planning menu items to keeping track of cash and charge receipts. The manager also place orders based on estimated food consumption, and then receives and checks the quantity and quality of all food and other deliveries. Food service managers—as well as executive chefs—also oversee all food preparation, cooking, and service, in addition to customer complaints and requests.

During a typical day, food service managers must handle matters as wide-ranging as equipment maintenance, sanitation, pest control, and security. They may also have some administrative duties, including keeping records of employees' hours and wages, preparing the payroll, and doing all the paperwork involved in keeping track of taxes, Social Security, and unemployment compensation. Some food service managers may have the assistance of a bookkeeper, as well as computer software to keep track of employee schedules, sales, inventory, and specific menu items. By the end of the day, however, when the day's receipts have been secured or deposited, ovens and lights have been turned off and alarm systems turned on, food service managers have more than earned their pay.

Two-Year Training

More than 800 two-year colleges, technical institutes, and other institutions offer programs in restaurant and food service management. Colleges that offer opportunities for on-the-job training through internship programs are especially desirable. While working on an associate's degree, food service manager candidates should take courses that will develop their skills in food production and preparation, business management, and leadership and supervisory skills. Most food service management programs offer instruction in those areas, plus courses in nutrition, food standards and sanitation, and food cost accounting.

Students should also look for courses that will help them stand out as a job candidate. These include classes in safety and sanitation, food purchasing, beverage management, nutrition, speech, accounting, marketing, wines, catering and banquet management, business law, or business correspondence, and computer applications such as EGS F&B (the program from Enggist & Grandjean Software for tracking food and beverage inventory) and similar software that monitors food and beverage inventory, orders, and costs. Other generally helpful classes for the food-service manager are psychology, economics, and chemistry.

As entry-level food service managers pursue their careers, they will find it to their advantage to seek additional certification according to their experience and interests. There are more than 50 such degrees and certificates in the food service field. Among the most desirable certificates is the FMP (food management professional) certificate from the National Restaurant Association Educational Foundation. These are awarded to managers who complete a series of courses in food service management, meet standards of work experience, and pass a written exam. Though not always a requirement for employment, the FMP certificate shows that a food service manager is serious about his or her work and credentials.

What to Look For in a School

Be sure to ask these important questions when looking for a two-year school.

☞ Will the school teach me the basic skills in culinary arts and food service management?

☞ Will I learn additional skills in such fields as business, software use, and psychology that will make me a stronger job candidate?

☞ Will the school help me find internships?

☞ What kinds of jobs do the school's graduates land, and what is the school's job placement rate?

☞ Does the school have courses in the areas of culinary arts and food service management that interest me?

☞ What are the professors' credentials and experience?

☞ What are the kitchens and classroom facilities like? Is the equipment up to date?

Interview with a Professional: Q&A

Sean O'Brien

Executive chef, Myth, San Francisco

Q: *How did you get started?*

A: My goal was to study business. Then I realized one day that much of my free time was devoted to my "hobby" of cooking. So I decided to try to turn it into a career. In school I was driven enough to get an internship at a high-end, four-star hotel.

Q: *What's a typical day like?*

A: We're open for dinner only five nights a week. I come in at 1 p.m. and leave at 1 or 2 a.m. It's a long day, but I love what I do. I oversee all aspects of the food creation process. But there are other managerial aspects as well, such as hiring, firing, payroll, dealing with potential suppliers, or doing off-site events. I check the reservation sheet to see if any VIPs are coming, if there are any special requests, dietary concerns, birthdays, and so on. I assist everyone to make sure they and their station are ready for service by 5:30 p.m. During the dinner service, I will "float" to help out and make sure everything goes out the way I intended it to go out. I also try to spend time in creating new dishes, to keep my customers (and myself) interested and keep customers coming back.

Q: *What's your advice for those starting a career?*

A: Talk to friends, family, teachers and find out who they know in the field. Talk to these contacts about their jobs. Spend a day in a bookstore looking at cookbooks. Go to your favorite restaurant and see if they will let you observe what goes on behind the scenes.

Q: *What's the best part of being an executive chef?*

A: What I create is edible art. It utilizes all five senses. This job is not necessarily about money, because in the beginning, it is a struggle. But in the end, you're getting paid to enjoy your hobby. And the smile on your guests' faces is payment, too!

The Future

Jobs for food service managers are expected to increase as the population grows, and options will be good for those with a bachelor's or associate's degree in food service management. Opportunities should be especially bright in the institutional food service area, such as hospitals, nursing homes, and assisted living facilities. However, the hiring for those facilities is likely to be managed by big food service companies. Anyone concerned with advancement may want to seek jobs in restaurants that are affiliated with national or regional chains because this is where the growth is currently greatest in the restaurant industry. He or she should also be willing to relocate if promoted, since this is the typical route to advancement.

Did You Know?

More than four out of 10 adults have worked in the restaurant industry at some time during their lives and over one out of every four adults got their first job experience in a restaurant.

Job Seeking Tips

✔ Research the restaurant business and decide what aspects interest you.

✔ Build a résumé or portfolio that shows a variety of learning and work experiences.

✔ Join organizations or take part in activities where you will meet people who may be able to advise you on your career.

✔ Talk to the career placement office to find out what career paths within the restaurant industry are available.

✔ See Appendix A for tips on creating a résumé, interviewing for schools or jobs, and collecting references.

Career Connections

For further information, contact the following organizations.

The **National Restaurant Association Educational Foundation** sponsors the ProStart Career Path program for high school juniors and seniors, which has enrolled over 45,000 high school juniors and seniors in programs studying restaurant and food service management. http://www.nraef.org

The **American Culinary Federation**runs an apprenticeship program for more than 2,000 students. Its online site provides certification prep courses and a practice certification test.   http://www.acfchefs.org

The **Society for Foodservice Management** publishes an online training manual for food service students.   http://www.sfm-online.org

Associate's Degree Programs

Here are a few schools offering quality food service management programs:

College of DuPage, Glen Ellyn, Illinois

Orange Coast College, Costa Mesa, California

Central Florida Community College, Ocala, Florida

Newbury College, Brookline, Massachusetts

Westchester Community College, Valhalla, New York

Financial Aid

Here are a few sources for scholarships and aid relating to food service management. For more on financial aid for two-year students, see the restaurant associations in each state as well as Appendix B of this book.

The **National Restaurant Association Educational Foundation** awards $2,000 scholarships to students in the restaurant and food service industry.   http://www.nraef.org

The **American Hotel & Lodging Educational Foundation** awards scholarships to students enrolled in hospitality management programs, culinary arts, and tourism administration. http://www.ahlef.org

The **Canadian Hospitality Foundation** awards about $120,000 each year in Canada to students pursuing careers in the food service and hospitality industry.   http://www.chfscholarships.com

Related Careers

Lodging manager, manager of food preparation and service workers, chef, executive chef, dining room manager, and banquet manager.

Dietetic
Technician

Vital Statistics

Salary: The median yearly wages of a dietetic technician are about $27,040, according to 2006 data from the U.S. Bureau of Labor Statistics.

Employment: New jobs for dietetic technicians will grow at about an average rate through 2014. About 8,000 additional employees will be added to the 25,000 employees now working in the field.

Education: This position requires an associate's degree, vocational school training, or on-the-job experience.

Work Environment: Dietetic technicians work in a wide range of health-care and educational environments as well as for community agencies that provide nutrition education.

Have you ever stood in line at your school cafeteria and asked yourself, "Who plans the menus for all these meals"? The answer may well be a dietetic technician. While not a full-blown dietician or a nutritionist (for which a bachelor's degree is required), the dietetic technician assists the dietician and plays a key role in the planning and delivery of meals. Dietetic technicians also order food, observe and assess dietary needs, and counsel and educate consumers so they will chose foods that are best suited to their particular health needs.

Dietetic technicians work in a wide variety of settings including schools, hospitals, nursing homes, senior citizen centers, Meals on Wheels programs, and even prisons. You'll find them in colleges and universities as well as in businesses and industries. What's more you'll find dietetic technicians assisting in weight-control clinics, athletic training facilities, food-service management firms, and government agencies. They may help community dieticians in senior feeding programs; the Special Supplemental Nutrition Program for Women, Infants, and Children (WIC)—the main food subsidy for poor people in the United States; public health departments; and day care centers.

In some ways dietetic technicians and food service managers provide a similar service: Both plan menus and supervise food production. However, food service managers serve food that people *want* to eat, whether or not a particular food is always good for them, while the dietetic technician's goal is to serve food that a particular group *needs* to eat for nutritional reasons.

Since 1906 when vitamins were first discovered, huge strides have been made in our knowledge of healthy eating and the role proper diet and nutrition plays in our lives. Along with other advances, this knowledge has helped to increase the average lifespan of Americans from 49 in 1901 to 77 today. Dietetic technicians can rightly take part of the credit for this remarkable achievement.

Despite this progress, however, there is still vast room for improvement in the American diet. For instance, two-thirds of American adults are now overweight, and one-third of all American children are now overweight or in danger of becoming so. Diabetes, a disease that can be at least partly controlled by diet, has also shown an alarming increase in recent years—up 33 percent between 1990 and 2000. Dietetic technicians are in a key position to improve this situation.

Today there are about 25,000 dietetic technicians in the United States, and they have a surprisingly broad influence on what millions of Americans eat every day. Suppose the average dietetic technician serves meals to 500 people a day—not an unreasonable assumption given the large size of many schools, hospitals, and other institutions—that's more than 12 million people a day whose diet is at least in part determined by dietetic technicians.

After completing an associate's degree as dietetic technicians, the graduate is eligible to take a national registration exam. Those who pass then receive the dietetic technician registered (DTR) credential. That title is a calling card to a career where one's efforts can really make a difference in the length and quality of other people's lives.

> ### "Tell me what you eat, and I will tell you what you are."
> —Anthelme Brillat-Savarin (1755–1826), French lawyer, politician, and gourmet

On the Job

Being a dietetic technician involves not only feeding many, many people nutritious meals on a daily basis, but also being able to instill smart nutrition habits in those clients. As a dietetic technician, you may not be in charge of your institution's whole dining operation, but your assistance to the head dietician is vital in determining whether your diner has a healthful dining experience.

In preparing meals you'll need math and organizational skills to determine the right quantities of food to use in recipes, and communication skills to supervise others who are producing or serving those meals. When working directly with clients to monitor their food intake, you'll need strong observational and reporting skills. You also may use computer programs to track your client's health status and nutritional needs and intake. You may input important information such as food allergies, special orders, and other information such as how a patient's diet may affect their medications.

If you counsel clients on good nutrition habits, you'll be calling on your abilities as a teacher and your powers of persuasion. You'll need those skills too when you introduce new clients to the principles of nutrition.

When you're not dealing directly with your consumers and assisting in the planning and production of meals, you may be choosing, scheduling, and conducting in-service programs for other food workers. In addition, you may be assisting the head dietician in researching food, nutrition, and food-service systems, as well as in developing job requirements, job descriptions, and work schedules.

Keys to Success

To be a successful dietetic technician, you should have (a) strong
- communication skills
- understanding of sound nutrition principles
- ability to cooperate
- problem-solving skills
- desire to provide nutritious, good-tasting meals

Do You Have What It Takes?

Students interested in careers as dietetic technicians should have not only a strong interest in food, but also a deep desire to help others lead healthier lives. Most people are willing to accept nutrition advice from a professional. Others, however, find it difficult to change their ways of eating in order to improve their health. For these people, dietetic technicians need to call on a depth of knowledge as well as their skills and persuasive powers to convince a patient to change bad eating habits. Future dietetic technicians can develop their knowledge base by taking courses like biology, home economics, and mathematics and joining organizations like 4-H. They can also hone their powers of persuasion by joining the school debating society. In addition, they can gain valuable experience by volunteering at a local hospital or nursing home.

How to Break In

Opportunities for dietetic technicians should keep pace with the average increase in the labor market over the next five years. Anyone starting out in this field, however, can increase his or her chances of breaking in with the following steps. First, focus the job search on contract providers of food services, such as Sysco or U.S. Performance, as well as outpatient-care centers, where employment for dietetic technicians is expected to grow more rapidly. Second, consider taking specialized courses in diet for diabetic or renal (kidney-related) patients. That's because Medicare coverage may be expanding to include nutrition therapy for these conditions. So opportunities should increase for dietetic technicians who are trained in managing these illnesses through dietary changes.

A Typical Day at Work

A typical day for a DTR is centered on assisting the registered dietician in the planning and production of menus for the needs of a regular clientele. The type of institution—school, rehabilitation center, senior citizen center, or county jail, just to name a few—will determine whether a dietetic technician has to plan one, two, or three meals a day.

Early in the morning, menus previously planned are put into production for the day. Later in the morning DTRs may assist dieticians in figuring out the amount of food and beverages that will need to be ordered for future menus. They may work together also to determine food costs and put cost-control procedures in place, so they don't spend more on food than they have in their budgets. Additionally DTRs may plan the work schedules for food service workers or determine the tasks that the workers will need to do. For most DTRs, however, the better part of the day is spent assisting the registered dietician in the preparation, production, and service of the food on the menus they have planned.

When they're not focusing on the above activities, many DTRs are involved in activities such as reporting on patient food intake, or in getting and evaluating dietary histories of clients in order to plan nutritional programs that fit their specific needs. DTRs may round out their day with a check to see that all the food that is planned for the next day's meals is ready to be prepared when needed. DTRs may also check to make sure that all the needed workers are on the next day's schedule.

Two-Year Training

Students interested in this field can choose from among almost 60 accredited two-year programs. These dietary programs, which have been approved by the American Dietetic Association, include least 450 hours of supervised practice in food-service management. Though there is some leeway in what training each program offers, most of the programs include courses that cover basic educational requirements as well as physical and biological sciences, such as biology, microbiology, or biochemistry; and physiology and anatomy.

Food and nutrition courses are also emphasized, of course. Students study food-service management, normal nutrition, and medical nutrition. They also focus on sanitation management, healthcare management and supervision, and principals of human resources.

Colleges may also offer courses in areas as diverse as community nutrition and food availability, cultural considerations in food preparation, and medical terminology. By taking an accredited program, upon graduation students will be able to evaluate patients' nutritional needs; maintain food procurement systems; plan menus for normal and modified diets; educate patients about nutrition; and monitor diets for quality.

Graduates of these programs receive the DTR credential when they pass a national assessment test. The credential, which must be updated very five years, is a huge door-opener for jobs.

What to Look For in a School

When considering a two-year school, be sure to ask these questions:

☞ Will the school teach me the basic skills to become a dietetic technician?

☞ Will I become familiar with such subjects as food-service management, nutrition therapy, and sanitation management?

☞ What kinds of jobs do the school's graduates land, and what is the school's job placement rate?

☞ Does the school offer courses in those aspects of the dietetic technician's career that interest me?

☞ What sort of internships and hands-on experience can I get?

☞ What are the professors' credentials and experience? Have they worked in the industry?

☞ What are the laboratories and classroom facilities like? Is the equipment up to date?

The Future

Dietetic technicians can expect average growth in their occupation through 2012. Spurring job growth is an increasing emphasis on preventing disease and improving diet. There's also an increased demand for nutritional information. What's more, the increase in the number of elderly will mean a greater demand for nutritional services in assisted living facilities. (However, this trend may be balanced out by a growth in the number of institutions that contract their food services with outside agencies.) Employment of dietetic technicians in such settings as food-service–provided institutions, out-patient-care centers, and the offices of physicians and other healthcare providers seems to be on the rise. Finally, employment opportunities should exist for those dietetic technicians who have specialized training in treating patients in diabetes management and the nutritional care of other conditions.

Interview with a Professional:
Q&A
Stacey Henderson
Dietetic technician registered, Americare Health and Rehabilitation Center, Memphis, Tennessee

Q: *How did you get started?*

A: As a teenager I had worked at a deli and gradually worked my way up to management. I was always particular about correct food temperature, proper hygiene, and sanitation. I wanted to learn more, so I applied for dietetic technician school.

Q: *What's a typical day like?*

A: Working in a long-term care facility, my job responsibilities include: nutrition assessments; monitoring residents who require wound therapy, are on therapeutic diets, or have had weight variances. I also make recommendations for nutrition interventions, assist the Registered Dietitian with oral feeding regimens, communicate with nursing staff regarding residents' nutritional status, and attend family care–plan meetings.

Q: *What's your advice for those starting a career?*

A: Learn both food-service management and clinical nutrition, even if you desire to concentrate in only one of these areas. Participate in continuing education and get involved in extracurricular activities, local dietetic groups, and so on. This allows you to meet others in the profession and keeps your skills up to date.

Q: *What's the best part of being a dietetic technician?*

A: The best part is the option to go into food-service management or clinical nutrition. As a dietetic technician, career opportunities are available in a variety of settings including hospitals, long-term care facilities and restaurants. This is a great career for those who enjoy working with and helping people.

Did You Know?

The first known written dietary advice is from a Babylonian stone tablet dating from 2500 B.C.E.: "If a man has pain inside . . . let him refrain from eating onions for three days."

Job Seeking Tips

✔ Join groups and take part in activities where you will meet people who may be able to advise you on your career.

✔ Decide in what setting you would prefer to work—hospital, senior citizen center, and so on—and seek relevant information and experience.

✔ Talk to the career placement office to find out what career paths are available within the nutrition therapy field.

✔ See Appendix A for tips on creating a résumé, interviewing for schools or jobs, and collecting references.

Career Connections

For further information, contact the following organizations.

The **American Diabetes Association** is the nation's leading organization for diabetes information. Especially recommended are its "Resources for Professionals." http://www.diabetes.org

The **American Dietetic Association** is the largest organization of food and nutrition professionals, and offers student memberships and networking opportunities. This organization also accredits dietetic technician programs. http://www.eatright.org

The **American Obesity Association (AOA)** provides education, research, and advocacy for treating and curing obesity. http://www.obesity.org

The **Center for Science in the Public Interest** is a nonprofit education and advocacy group whose goal is to improve the safety and nutritional quality of our food supply. It publishes the excellent *Nutrition Action Newsletter*. http://www.cspinet.org

Associate's Degree Programs

Here are a few colleges offering quality dietetic technician programs. All are accredited by the American Dietetic Association.

Baltimore City Community College, Baltimore, Maryland

Milwaukee Area Technical College, Milwaukee, Wisconsin

Southern Maine Community College, South Portland, Maine

Southwest Tennessee Community College, Memphis, Tennessee

Tarrant County College, Arlington, Texas

Truckee Meadows Community College, Reno, Nevada

Financial Aid

Here are a few food- and nutrition-related scholarships. Remember also to check state and local dietetic associations and food-related organizations. For more on financial aid for two-year students, turn to Appendix B.

The **American Dietetic Association Foundation (ADAF)** offers a variety of scholarships and stipends to individuals pursuing an undergraduate degree in dietetics or a food- or nutrition-related subject. Some of these scholarships are earmarked for students in the second year of a dietetic technician program. For more information, see their Web site at http://www.eatright.org.

The **National Future Farmers of American Organization (FFA)** offers over $2 million in scholarships to undergraduates who are studying food science and other farm-related subjects. The applicant must be a member of the FFA.   http://www.ffa.org/programs/scholarships

Related Careers

Dietician, nutritionist, food service manager, health educator, and registered nurse.

Environmental Science and Protection Technician

Vital Statistics

Salary: Average earnings for environmental technicians are about $35,800 a year, according to 2006 data from the U.S. Bureau of Labor Statistics.

Employment: Employment opportunities in this field are growing at an average to above-average rate.

Education: Either two years of specialized training or a two-year associate's degree is necessary. Some employers, however, prefer a four-year science degree or several science and math courses at a four-year college.

Work Environment: Environmental science and protection technicians work both outside in the field and in the laboratory to monitor environmental resources.

You may have seen movies such as Erin Brockovich, in which a legal assistant tracks down technical evidence to bring down a big polluter. The evidence, water quality results, was probably gathered by that unsung hero—an environmental science and protection technician.

Environmental science and protection technicians focus on monitoring, analyzing, and removing hazardous wastes and substances from places where they may endanger public health. These substances include asbestos, industrial wastewater pollutants, and dangerous chemicals and gases.

Given the wide variety of jobs related to the environment, it's not surprising that the same job title—environmental technician—can have a completely different meaning depending on where the job takes place. For example, in an engineering firm that specializes in constructing water treatment plants, an environmental technician may be someone who helps prepare statements that describe how a new treatment plant will affect the surrounding communities. In a hospital, an environmental technician may handle biological and radioactive wastes—a completely different job, yet one that is still related to the environment.

So when you come across references to environmental jobs, perhaps the best rule of thumb is not to go by the job title but rather by the job description. Find out what environmental science and protection technicians in your local city or local engineering firm actually do as part of the job. Then you'll be in a much better position to decide whether this job might actually be one for you.

The Bureau of Labor Statistics of the U.S. Department of Labor estimates that there are about 31,000 environmental science and protection technicians working in the United States. Most of them are employed by state and local governments as well as by professional, scientific, and technical services firms. What's more, in an effort to promote security against terrorist threats, local governments and private firms are gearing up to promote swift, effective, and efficient environmental cleanups. To do this, they need environmental technicians. So whether they work in the public or private sector, these individuals have the great satisfaction of knowing that they are protecting the environment and the public.

On the Job

Suppose a freight train running near your town has derailed and a tank car carrying a toxic liquid has burst open, spilling the dangerous substance on the ground. As an environmental science and protection technician in your state's Department of Environmental Protection, you hurry to the site of the accident, don a hazmat suit (designed to protect you from contact with hazardous materials), measure the amount of toxins spilled, and assist in the cleanup.

On a more routine day, you might take water samples from the source of the local drinking water supply and test them for purity. Or you might issue a violation notice to a local industrial supplier that has been illegally dumping solid waste. You could be providing testimony in a case brought against a polluter, or you could be assisting with the inspection of a solid waste facility to make sure it meets state requirements.

When you're not out in the field, you are in the office recording test data, preparing reports on data you've collected, or maintaining equipment used to measure different kinds of pollution. In short, the job of an environmental science and protection technician is a varied one. What's more, as there is no shortage of pollutants, monitoring and managing them should keep you pretty busy.

Environmental science and protection technicians use a variety of measuring devices and technical software to come up with information that environmental scientists can use to make decisions. For instance, environmental technicians working during the Hurricane Katrina cleanup operations used bioaerosol impactors. These are devices used to measure the presence of bacteria and fungi in both indoor and outdoor air. Other devices measure the particulate material in the air or analyze the toxicity of water.

Environmental science and protection technicians must also be familiar with the laws and regulations that apply where they operate. For example, did you know that it is illegal under the Refuse Act of 1899 to throw or deposit refuse of any kind into any navigable water, or tributary, of the United States? Environmental technicians know that law, because they are responsible for collecting evidence used to bring charges against violators.

Keys to Success

To be a successful environmental technician, you should have (a) strong

- knowledge of water, air, and solid waste contaminants
- science background
- attention to detail
- concern for safety precautions
- ability to track and organize data and use software
- reasoning and problem-solving skills

A Typical Day at Work

As an environmental science and protection technician, you would generally spend the day either assessing environmental quality or providing services when the environment is contaminated or degraded in some way.

On a typical morning, you go over questionnaires filled out by local industries that describe: the system they use to store fuel oil or other hazardous substances; the devices they use to measure air and water quality in their facilities; and the methods they use to dispose of their solid waste and other byproducts. In the afternoon, you head out in the field, don a hazmat suit, and measure the amount of a hazardous substance in the ground, air, or water in preparation for its removal. Toward the end of the day you fill out reports on your activities of that day, consult with your team members on the next steps for cleanup, or research the hazardous substance spill that you are scheduled to investigate the next day.

Though you often work outdoors, exposed to environmental hazards, you face little personal dangers because you follow proper safety procedures. For instance, you know that when dousing a fire that's burning a flammable substance, using water instead of foam may make the fire burn hotter. You also know which type of hazmat suit to wear for a particular chemical spill. This can save money as well as lives, because a hazmat suit costs as much as $1,000 and generally can be worn only once.

Do You Have What It Takes?

Do you enjoy solving problems and unlocking mysteries? Are you interested in being on the front lines in monitoring the environment? Do you think you have what it takes to assist in the cleanup of a toxic substance? Then consider a career as an environmental science and protection technician. Budding science technicians should have an interest in science and math and feel comfortable working in a laboratory. Strong computer skills are also necessary, as are communication skills and teamwork. In addition, the willingness to collect and organize large amounts of data and to find patterns in that data is a common characteristic of successful environmental technicians. Another common trait is a strong belief in the importance of keeping the environment safe from contamination or degradation and in preserving the public's safety from ingesting toxic substances.

How to Break In

Environmental science and protection technicians tend to be both knowledgeable and passionate about their professions. So start now building your base of knowledge about the environment, and take part in activities that demonstrate your commitment. Put extra effort into high school and college biology, ecology, chemistry, and other science courses. If you have the opportunity, attend any summer science camp programs and the conferences of professional organizations. Do volunteer work for scientific organizations, the science department of your local college or any environmental groups or nature centers. Join environmental organizations. The experience you'll gain not only will give you an edge when seeking full-time positions, it will provide you with a network of contacts who can help steer you towards employment.

> **"Don't wait for your 'dream job' to appear in the classifieds. Solicit companies you would like to work for and be persistent. Be willing to accept an entry-level position."**
> —Reagan A. Jones, environmental manager, HAZ-M.E.R.T.

Two-Year Training

More than a hundred two-year colleges offer programs in environmental technology. While the emphasis may vary from program to program, you'll find a common core of subjects. These include college algebra, chemistry, computer applications, biology, introductory environmental science, soil science, air quality, water quality, technical writing, environmental regulation, and hazardous matter operations. You may also have the opportunity to take courses in geology, mapping, surveying, GIS (geographic information systems) and GPS (global positioning systems), and environmental site assessment.

Many jobs in this field also require certification, usually by professional associations such as the National Environmental Health Association or the Institute for Hazardous Materials Management. These certificates enable you to step right into many jobs where certification is required. For instance, students who take a course in hazardous waste operations may receive the federal Occupational Health and Safety Administration (OSHA) certificate in this subject as a part of their coursework. So research any certifications you may want to achieve and take courses that will give you the eligibility.

As you research programs, you'll find that some schools count internships as part of the curriculum; others don't mention them. In either case, build up as much on-the-job experience as you can in areas of interest while you're in school. Also, keep in mind that environmental science and protection technology is an evolving field. You may need periodic refresher courses to keep up to speed.

What to Look For in a School

When considering a two-year school, be sure to ask these questions:

☞ Will the school teach me the basic skills in environmental science and protection?

☞ Will I become familiar with such subjects as air and water pollution abatement, GPS, hazardous waste regulations, toxicology, and computer applications?

☞ What kinds of jobs do the school's graduates land, and what is the school's job-placement rate?

☞ Does the school offer courses in those aspects of environmental science and protection that interest me?

☞ What are the professors' credentials and experience? Have they worked in the environmental science industry?

☞ What are the laboratories and classroom facilities like? Is the equipment up to date?

The Future

Through 2014 job growth for environmental science and protection technicians is expected to be as fast as the field has averaged in recent years. The public continues to show high levels of environmental concern, especially in the light of continued evidence of the effects of global warming and environmental degradation. As the population increases and energy prices rise, increased efforts to promote clean energy alternatives and energy conservation will require more workers to regulate and recycle waste products, enforce environmental regulations, and clean up toxic waste sites. What's more, security efforts to prevent environmental terrorist episodes should spur the hiring of environmental technicians.

Interview with a Professional: *Q&A*

Reagan A. Jones
Environmental manager, HAZ-M.E.R.T, Inc.,
Rogers, Arkansas

Q: *How did you get started?*

A: I knew my career needed to be in a field that I was personally passionate about. While enrolled in the environmental program at my community college, I applied for an internship with the local solid waste district. There I was able to expose myself to other local environmental agencies and businesses and to participate in community environmental events. All of these provided networking opportunities. When my internship was nearing completion I was offered a part-time position with a county environmental office, where I worked for the year until I graduated. Then I was offered a full-time management position with a private environmental firm. Little did I know when accepting the original internship that it would provide the exposure and networking opportunities that led to my dream career.

Q: *What's a typical day like?*

A: I manage scheduled projects such as environmental audits and asbestos surveys. I also handle environmental emergencies that require immediate attention. Having such varied job duties allows for a combination of desk work, research, and fieldwork. Emergencies must be handled 24/7, 365 days a year.

Q: *What's your advice for those starting a career?*

A: Be active in the community you live in or want to work in. Don't wait for your "dream job" to appear in the classifieds. Solicit companies you would like to work for and be persistent. Be willing to accept an entry-level position. Once you have your foot in the door, demonstrate that whatever the task is, you can be counted on to see it through.

Q: *What's the best part about being an environmental manager?*

A: Every day I truly feel like I am making a positive environmental impact in my community and getting paid for it!

Job Seeking Tips

✔ Volunteer or look for internships with local organizations that do environmental work.

✔ Decide what specific area of the environment you're interested in and seek relevant experience.

✔ Talk to the career placement office.

✔ Join local environmental organizations or attend conferences, lectures or other events that will help you meet other people in your field.

✔ See Appendix A for tips on creating a résumé, interviewing for schools or jobs, and collecting references.

Did You Know?

In 1980 Congress established the Superfund to clean up the nation's worst toxic waste sites. Since then, release of toxic wastes has been successfully controlled at over 900 of the 1,500 most dangerous sites.

Career Connections

For further information, contact the following organizations.

The Environmental Careers Organization (ECO) has an extensive list of paid internships on its Web site.   http://www.eco.org

The federal **Environmental Protection Agency** lists internships and other employment possibilities for students, in particular its Student Career Experience Program (SCEP) and Student Temporary Employment Program (STEP). Click on Careers, then Student Opportunities. http://www.epa.gov

The **National Resources Defense Council**, a well-established advocacy organization, has an excellent site that features up-to-date news on environmental topics and has extensive links to other related Web sites. http://www.nrdc.org

Associate's Degree Programs

Clover Park Technical College, Lakewood, Washington

Delaware Technical and Community College, Stanton and Wilmington, Delaware

NorthWest Arkansas Community College, Bentonville, Arkansas

Schoolcraft College, Livonia, Michigan

Texas State Technical College West Texas, Breckenridge, Texas

Three Rivers Community College Mohegan Campus, Norwich, Connecticut

Financial Aid

Here is information about environmental science and protection–related scholarships. For financial aid for two-year students, turn to Appendix B. Students are encouraged to look especially for scholarships offered by state departments of environmental protection.

The **Hispanic Scholarship Fund Institute**, supported by the U.S. Department of Energy, offers $2,000 scholarships to two-year college students pursuing majors related to environmental restoration and waste management.   http://www.hsfi.org

Related Careers

Environmental compliance inspector, soil scientist, food science technician, chemical technician, forensic science technician, occupational health and safety specialist, and chemical equipment controller and operator.

Water or Wastewater Treatment Plant Operator

Vital Statistics

Salary: The median yearly salary of a water or wastewater treatment plant operator is about $34,960, according to 2006 data from the U.S. Bureau of Labor Statistics.

Employment: Opportunities are expected to grow at an average rate until 2012. Job openings will outnumber job applicants.

Education: This position usually requires an associate's degree and on-the-job experience. As larger, more complex treatment plants are built, educational requirements may increase.

Work Environment: Water and wastewater treatment plant operators work both inside and outside, sometimes in tight or otherwise uncomfortable conditions.

You may not think much about the water that comes out of your faucet, or what happens to the wastewater from your toilet or bathtub. Local governments, however, think a great deal about these things. In fact, water and wastewater treatment plant operators are some of the most important people on the front lines of the war against environmental pollution. They act as gatekeepers of the nation's water supply and navigable waterways. They protect these resources—and us—from pollutants that could poison us, harm our quality of life, and damage the fish and wildlife that also depend on clean water to survive. Industries treat the water they use in their manufacturing processes to remove pollutants before returning it to the environment. So they rely on water and wastewater treatment operators too.

Water treatment plant operators make drinking water safe by treating it with chemicals and filtering out impurities. Wastewater treatment plant operators remove pollutants from both domestic and industrial liquid waste so that it can be safely returned to the environment. Though they work in different facilities, both water treatment and wastewater treatment plant operators control the equipment and processes that treat water.

There are about 170,000 water and wastewater treatment systems in the United States, and almost 100,000 plant operators run them. Almost four in five of them work for local governments. Most of the rest work for private water and sewage treatment facilities and for private waste-management services. Both wastewater and water treatment plants may operate with as few as one part-time employee, as in many rural areas, or dozens of workers, as in a typical municipal plant. Plant size is determined by the size of the population it serves, as well as the number of industries in the area that use water in their manufacturing processes. Since most water or waste-water treatment plants run 24 hours a day, seven days a week, employees work in shifts, as in a factory. As in any factory, there is security in place to protect the industry from sabotage, but security may be tighter at larger water treatment plants because of the potential danger to the public health from an act of terrorism.

Since clean water is an absolute necessity for healthy human life, there will always be a demand for skilled water treatment plant operators. Mean-while communities in some parts of the West and Southwest face concerns about potential water shortages and a growing number of chemicals are monitored in the water. So the water treatment plant operator's job may become even more important in protecting the public health. With this in-creased responsibility, however, comes greater career satisfaction. Water treatment plant operators know that because they are on the job, the pub-lic doesn't have to be concerned about their health every time they turn on a water tap.

> **"Demand for qualified water treatment operators is high. And the need for clean water is not going to go away."**
> —Neil Stocker, water plant operations supervisor

On the Job

Almost all the water used in homes, and most of that used in business and industry, goes through local water treatment plants (which are usu-ally smaller than wastewater facilities). Before water flows into the home, the water treatment plant operator removes any impurities and usually adds chlorine so that the water is drinkable and fluoride to protect the public's teeth.

Meanwhile wastewater coming into the typical treatment plant under-goes as many as four kinds of treatment before it is released into a river, stream, or reservoir. The wastewater treatment plant operator plays an ac-tive role in each of these phases of treatment. He or she monitors these processes by reading, analyzing, and adjusting the controls of huge filtering systems. The operators may step in when there's a breakdown or the system needs maintenance. They are responsible both for the removal of harmful substances from the water and for the maintenance of the equipment.

On the job chemistry is used when operators adjust the amount of chlorine and other chemicals used in filtering the water. It's also used to analyze water samples. Careful observational skills are essential also. Operators monitor the pipes and pumps that control the flow of liquid and make sure everything is working properly. When the equipment is malfunctioning, they use their mechanical skills and training to figure out what's wrong and fix the machinery. Sometimes operators find themselves in emergency situations. Then they use special safety equipment and act quickly to protect the public health. Since the number of contaminants that must be controlled in our water supply has grown over time, they must also be familiar with the latest regulations and how they affect their particular plant. It's a big responsibility, and one that water treatment plant operators take seriously.

Keys to Success

To be a successful water treatment operator you should have (a) strong

- technical know-how
- skills in operating, and repairing machines or systems
- problem-solving skills
- understanding of chemistry and laboratory methods
- observation and communication skills
- commitment to superior water quality

Do You Have What It Takes?

If you hope to become a water and wastewater treatment plant operator, you should be handy with machines and tools. You should also enjoy science, math, and computers. In addition, you should be able to stay calm in an emergency and work well under pressure. You'll need to be able to work alone as well as in groups and make decisions independently, especially in smaller treatment plants. Because treatment plants run 24 hours a day, you'll also need to be flexible about working at different times of the day and night.

How to Break In

While in high school, focus on math, chemistry, biology, and computer courses. Also take shop courses to gain familiarity with common tools and machines. When you move on to your two-year degree, aim for lots of hands-on training through field trips, lab courses, and internships. In the internships you'll probably work under an experienced operator doing routine tasks. He or she may be a job contact later on. Once you graduate you'll also need to be certified. The requirements vary from state to state, and there are different levels of certification.

Though it's possible to break into the field of water treatment as a trainee without a degree or certification, candidates with a two-year degree in water treatment plant operation have a serious edge. Larger plants especially give priority to hiring workers who have formal training or education in the field.

A Typical Day at Work

Operators usually start their shift by walking around the plant and checking to see whether any problems have cropped up. Then they control the pumps and valves that move the water or wastewater through the plant. They read the meters and make adjustments to ensure that all the plant equipment is operating correctly. They also control equipment that removes or destroys all the harmful materials in the water by treating it with chemicals like chlorine. In addition, plant operators take samples of the treated water, analyze them for purity, and make adjustments in the treatment. They repair pumps, valves, and other machinery; run tests on equipment; track their work; and monitor all or part of the whole operation, often by computer. Occasionally when sudden rainstorms create an overflow that exceeds the plant's capacity or a chlorine gas leak develops, operators step in and correct the situation. They have group meetings, sometimes daily, in which a supervisor coordinates the upcoming activities of the operators, maintenance staff, and any subcontractors.

Two-Year Training

There are more than 50 different one- or two-year college programs in water quality and wastewater treatment management. As federal, state, and local regulations that govern water quality become stricter, however, degree requirements may change. When investigating a particular school, it is best to call and speak to someone in the department that handles water quality courses.

Most of these programs offer classes in basic and advanced wastewater treatment technology as well as in chemistry. Required courses include water quality analysis also, emphasizing either the biological or instrumental sides of the subject. Other mainstays are courses on utility equipment control and utility management. You will almost always find courses on hydrology or hydraulics (both of which deal with different aspects of water and water flow). Finally, almost all of these programs require internships or job training.

What to Look For in a School

When evaluating a two-year school, be sure to ask these questions:

☞ Will the school teach me the basic skills in water- and wastewater treatment management?

☞ Will I become familiar with such subjects as chemistry, water quality analysis, hydrology, and computer applications?

☞ What kinds of jobs do the school's graduates land, and what is the school's job placement rate?

☞ Does the school offer courses in those aspects of wastewater and water treatment management that interest me?

☞ What are the professors' credentials and experience? Have they worked in the environmental science industry? Are they available outside the classroom and by e-mail?

☞ What are the laboratories and classroom facilities like? Is the equipment up to date?

The Future

Job growth for water and wastewater treatment operators is expected to be about average through 2014. Individuals who have training in the most aspects of water and wastewater treatment, and who can handle multiple duties, will have the broadest opportunities. Though most of the jobs are with local governments, job growth will be higher in the private sector. First, a growing number of local governments are likely to be hiring private firms to provide their operation and management services (due to increased federal certification requirements for operations). Second, a growing number of private industries are treating the water they use before it leaves their plants.

Did You Know?

Although 70 percent of the earth's surface is covered with water, 97 percent of it is salt water. Another 2 percent is glacier ice. Only 1 percent is fresh water.

Interview with a Professional:
Q&A
Neil Stocker
Water plant operations supervisor,
Cholla Water Treatment Plant, Glendale, Arizona

Q: *How did you get started?*

A: I was looking to make a career change, and my wife suggested waste-water treatment. Demand for qualified water treatment operators is high, and the need for clean water is not going to go away. After two years I received an A.A.S. [associate of applied science] degree in water purification technologies. An internship gave me the opportunity to get my feet wet, as it were, working at a city water treatment facility. Upon graduation I was immediately hired by a subcontractor to work at a Motorola facility in Phoenix to treat water for one of their processes.

Q: *What's a typical day like?*

A: Water plant operators are responsible for providing safe drinking water to the public based on Environmental Protection Agency [EPA] guidelines. During the shift an operator will monitor the plant; make adjustments to chemical doses to improve treatment; troubleshoot; and work in a lab doing tests for parameters such as pH [a measure of the range of saltiness or acidity], residual chlorine, alkalinity [having the properties of an alkali, or soluble salt], turbidity [cloudiness], temperature, conductivity, fluoride concentration, and hardness.

Q: *What's your advice for those starting a career?*

A: Look for a two-year college that offers formal training in the field of water treatment. In most states there are four to five levels of operator certification. While it is sometimes possible to get the first level of certification without education and/or experience, an associate's degree with internships typically gives you the education and experience to get to the higher certification level that most municipalities and private water companies require. Then a positive attitude goes a long way towards getting you in the door. Have the motivation to move forward and make a success of your choice.

Q: *What's the best part about being a water treatment plant supervisor?*

A: The satisfaction of knowing that I am doing something important for the community. I have a sense of pride and accomplishment in what I do.

Job Seeking Tips

✔ Look for ways to meet people who may help you with your job search.

✔ Decide what you're interested in and seek relevant experience.

✔ Talk to the career placement office.

✔ See Appendix A for tips on creating a résumé, interviewing for schools or jobs, and collecting references.

Career Connections

For further information contact the following organizations.

The **American Water Works Association** has a student center on its Web site that offers information on industry trends, scholarships, internships, and more.   http://www.awwa.org

The **National Onsite Wastewater and Recycling Association** promotes onsite wastewater treatment, recycling, and other activities through education and training.   http://www.nowra.org

The **Water Environment Federation** is an international technical and education organization whose purpose is to preserve and enhance the global water environment.   http://www.wef.org

The **Water Quality Association** is an international trade association representing the household, commercial, industrial, and small community water treatment industry.   http://www.wqa.org

Associate's Degree Programs

Here are a few schools offering quality water and wastewater treatment programs:

Delta College, University City, Michigan

GateWay Community College, Phoenix, Arizona

Green River Community College, Auburn, Washington

St. Cloud Technical College, St. Cloud, Minnesota

San Bernardino Valley College, San Bernardino, California

Financial Aid

For water-related scholarships, research your state departments of environmental protection. For more on financial aid for two-year students turn to Appendix B.

The **National Ground Water Association** offers tuition scholarships to two-year students studying water drilling.   http://www.ngwa.org

Related Careers

Chemical equipment or plant operator, science technician, gas and oil plant operator, power plant operator, distributor, and dispatcher, stationary engineer, and boiler operator.

Dairy Farm Manager

Vital Statistics

Salary: The median yearly salary for a dairy farm manager is about $32,292. However wages vary widely depending on a farm's size and its products, according to 2006 data from the U.S. Bureau of Labor Statistics.

Employment: The brightest job opportunities exist for small-scale farmers who have found market niches in organically raised cows (whose milk products are hormone-free); farmers belonging to agricultural cooperatives; and those who sell directly to consumers through farmers' markets.

Education: To excel in today's competitive market, dairy managers should have at least a two-year degree with an agriculture focus.

Work Environment: Both outside and indoors. Typical dairy farms today have hundreds, even thousands, of cows and highly mechanized operations.

Got milk? There are about 81,000 dairy operations in the United States today where that question can be answered with a resounding "Yes!" These dairy farms produce a whopping 19.7 billion gallons of milk a year. What's especially surprising is that while the number of dairy cows has decreased over the past 30 years, the number of pounds of milk produced has jumped by almost 50 percent. Though some of the increase is due to the use of controversial growth hormones, a great deal is also due to farm manager's increasing efficiency in managing larger herds.

Dairy farm managers' efficiency comes from both education and on-site training. Dairy managers rely on the production edge they get from studying agriculture techniques and processes. They also draw on the practical knowledge they gain from their farm experiences, preferably in a mentor relationship with a master dairy farmer. Good dairy managers also reach out to others in the industry for advice, networking opportunities, and memberships in dairy cooperative associations that will lower their production and marketing costs. (Cooperatives are businesses that are owned and controlled by the people who use their products or services. Today, dairy cooperatives not only process milk, but market and ship it as well.)

About 80 percent of dairy farmers own the land on which they farm. Only about 20 percent work for others. Either way, dairy managers not only have a passion to produce superior dairy products, they also have the knowledge, skills, and abilities to inspire others to achieve the same level of intensity. They must be able to keep up with the latest technological developments and turn on a dime to make changes that will improve their profits.

Perhaps more than most farm operations, dairying is a business with little margin for error. Any one of a number of faulty conditions—improperly fed cows, nonsterile milking machinery, poor pasteurization, inefficient transportation—is enough to ruin a batch of milk. But if the risks are high, the rewards are also great. As most dairy farmers will tell you, despite the hard work there is tremendous satisfaction in knowing that you are providing a product that is in high demand by the public because it is both nutritious and delicious.

> **"Growing up on a dairy farm, you certainly learn discipline and a commitment to purpose."**
> —Mike Johanns, U.S. Secretary of Agriculture

On the Job

Dairying requires specific physical abilities and mental know-how. For instance, physical strength is needed to move a balky cow into line or deliver a calf when there are complications at birth. Manual dexterity is required to handle the milking and cleaning machinery. Though milking cows and cleaning the dairy barn have now been largely automated, the dairy manager must still be able to operate and repair the sophisticated equipment. Dairy managers also need to be as punctual as the workers they manage because cows must be fed, watered, and milked on a regular schedule, rain or shine. Dairy managers must also be observant and quick thinking. They need to be able to prevent or ease the effects of accidents, disease, and other potentially cow-threatening problems by spotting high-risk conditions and stepping in appropriately. On large farms, dairy managers may delegate some or all of their responsibilities to others. Still, they must be so familiar with each task that they could fill in for a missing worker. On smaller farms, the dairy manager does all the jobs side by side with his coworkers.

Even when the cows have been milked and turned out to pasture, the dairy manager's job is only partly done. He or she must also take charge of routine maintenance jobs, such as mending fences and checking feed supplies. During the warmer months, to save money, most dairy farmers sow, grow, and harvest grain crops, which can provide feed for the cows year round. An average cow, for instance, eats 95 pounds of hay a day, so the dairy farm manager can save a lot of money growing hay. Finally there is the office work, including ordering supplies, monitoring prices that milk products are getting, paying bills, and arranging lines of credit to help the farm manage periods when it is short on cash. And just when a normal worker's day might be over, the dairy manager must get up and supervise, if not actually take part in, a second milking operation just like the morning one. So sheer physical stamina is perhaps the last of a long list of characteristics the successful dairy manager needs.

Keys to Success

To be a successful dairy farm manager, you need (a) strong
- knowledge of dairy-cow breeding and care
- passion for dairy farming and its lifestyle
- business judgment
- problem-solving skills
- managerial, planning, and organizational skills
- self-motivation

Do You Have What It Takes?

Students interested in being in dairy management should believe in the importance of producing delicious, nutritious, and healthy milk products. If you have also grown up on a farm or believe you would enjoy working on one, you may want to consider becoming a dairy production manager. Future members of this occupation should take high school courses in agriculture, math, business, science, and computers. They should also take part in Future Farmers of America or 4-H activities. They also need to develop both the physical stamina to work long hours, often outdoors, and the knowledge and dexterity necessary to operate and repair equipment.

Two-Year Training

Many colleges and universities offer two-year degrees in dairy husbandry and production, dairy science technology, or dairy management. While differing in emphasis from school to school, most departments of dairy science have a core program that includes animal breeding and health, calf care, dairy production, farm business management, and computer applications. The basic concepts in each course are also applied to real-life situations through field trips, lab exercises, interactions with industry representatives, and internships on farms. Schools normally have a working dairy center as part of their facilities, including a milking parlor and grazing center where students take part in hands-on demonstrations of all

aspects of dairying. Some of the skills taught in these sessions include artificial insemination, vaccination, milk culturing, and dehorning. At the end
of the program, as one school's description puts it, "graduates are prepared
to manage cows and people."

A Typical Day at Work

A dairy manager's day begins as early as 4 a.m.—when most Americans are
in dreamland. Cows have to be milked two or even three times a day, and
even with machines and around-the-barn pipelines to move the milk, it's
still hard work. The machines that milk cows consist of hoses, connections,
and pipes, all of which have to be kept germ-free. Once they're turned on,
the milk is sucked through the hoses into one big clear container, which
also must be monitored to ensure that the milk is clean and drinkable.

After the cows are milked, which may take several hours or more depending on the size of the herd, the manager supervises the cleaning of the
cow stalls and cow barns, and has the cow manure hauled to a storage tank.
Between milkings, dairy farm managers are also responsible for feeding the
animals and checking their health. Since dairy farms often grow most of
the grain their cows eat, dairy farm managers also take care of these crops.
They'll usually do this after their lunch hour and check on the feed supplies, mend machinery, and complete other farm chores. Around 4 p.m.
the milking and feeding cycle begins again. It's a long but rewarding day,
because dairy farm managers know they are producing a wholesome, essential product.

How to Break In

Many dairy farm managers grew up on a family farm, but others are attracted by the rural life style and the opportunity to produce a needed
product. There is no minimum educational requirement to perform most
of the dairy farm manager's tasks. Nevertheless, a two-year degree is the
minimum a modern dairy farm manager needs to acquire the skills to
make good business decisions in the complex world of agriculture. Working under the supervision of an experienced farmer is also advisable, even
for graduates of a two-year college program. This way the dairy farm man-
ager-in-training can learn to translate classroom theories into practical
skills. Such hands-on experience coupled with a solid academic background in farm management should prepare the trainee well for a career as
a dairy farm manager.

What to Look For in a School

Ask these questions when looking for a two-year school for this field:

☞ Will the school teach me the basic skills in dairy farm management and dairy science?

☞ Will I learn additional skills in marketing, computer applications, dairy breeding, agricultural economics, and soil science?

☞ Will the school be able to help me get internships and apprenticeships?

☞ What kinds of jobs do the school's graduates get, and what is the school's placement rate?

☞ What are the professors' credentials and experience? Have they worked in the dairy industry? Are they available outside the classroom and by e-mail?

☞ What are the classrooms and model farm facilities like? Is the equipment up to date?

The Future

Dairy farming, like agriculture in general, has become both more productive and more expensive. This situation, in which fewer workers produce more goods, can drive many small farmers out of business and decrease the demand for farm managers. More and more small-scale farms, however, have been able to buck this trend in several ways. Some small-scale dairy farmers have taken advantage of the increasing demand for organic products, which are grown without chemicals or, in the case of animals, growth hormones. Others make use of local farmers' markets to deal directly with urban and suburban consumers. These farmers' markets enable the seller to make more profit by eliminating the middleman. Finally, many small dairy farmers belong to marketing cooperatives that lower the farmer's marketing, processing, and transportation costs.

True, the market for agricultural workers in general is declining. Yet there is always a demand for knowledgeable, organized, quick-thinking, energetic dairy farm managers who can manage their animals and farms efficiently.

Did You Know?

The most productive dairy cows yield over 25 gallons of milk a day. That's the equivalent of 400 glasses.

Interview with a Professional:
Q&A

Aaron Schatz

Partner, Schatz Dairy Farms, Cresco, Iowa

Q: *How did you get started?*

A: All my life I have lived on our family dairy farm. I have always loved it. After I graduated from Northeast Iowa Community College, I got a job at a local dairy supply company but continued to work on my family's farm. Eight months later, I bought a herd of 40 cows for $80,000 and went into a partnership with my parents. I had to get two loans to help pay for the cows and other costs. When I went to the banker, I had to have everything figured out about how I was going to pay back the loan. I still kept my other job for the paycheck and health insurance. After eight months, however, things were going well enough that I could make ends meet just by farming.

Q: *What's a typical day like?*

A: It always starts with getting up at 4:30 a.m. and milking our herd of 120 cows. I spend most of the morning milking, feeding, and taking care of the cows. This includes treating injuries, vaccinating, and giving pregnancy tests. In the growing season, most of the rest of the day is spent taking care of the feed crops or doing other odds-and-ends jobs. In the winter we spend a lot more time working with the cows, keeping them bedded and dry and out of any bad weather. Then at 4:30 p.m. we begin milking again and usually finish the day up at 8:00 p.m.

Q: *What's your advice for those starting a career?*

A: Get a partner. Another way would be to get a job as a herdsman (someone who assists the dairy manager). You will learn a lot working for other people, and you don't have to learn it all with your own cows at your expense.

Q: *What' s the best part of being a dairy farm manager?*

A: I am my own boss. Another thing I really like is working outside, especially when the sun is just coming up.

Job Seeking Tips

✔ Seek job experience in different areas such as crop farming, veterinary science, business, and accounting.

✔ Talk to the career placement office at your college.

✔ Join organizations that will help you meet people who can assist you with your career.

✔ See Appendix A for tips on creating a résumé, interviewing for schools or jobs, and collecting references.

Career Connections

For further information, contact the following organizations.

The **Alternative Farming System Information Center National Agricultural Library USDA** http://www.nal.usda.gov/afsic

The **Appropriate Technology Transfer for Rural Areas National Sustainable Agriculture Information Service** http://www.attra.ncat.org

Both of the above organizations supply information on diversified agriculture, education, training, and community-supported agriculture, and the latter specifically publishes information on internships and apprenticeships.

The **National Dairy Shrine** promotes the dairy industry. They also award some scholarships.   http://www.dairyshrine.org

Future Farmers of America http://www.ffa.org

The **U.S. Department of Agriculture** supplies information on government education and research programs.   http://www.csrees.usda.gov

Associate's Degree Programs

Here are a few schools that offer quality dairy science or dairy management programs:

Linn-Benton Community College, Albany, Oregon

Modesto Junior College, Modesto, California

Northeast Iowa Community College, Calmar, Iowa

State University of New York, Morrisville, New York

Financial Aid

Look here for dairy-related scholarships. For more on financial aid for two-year students, turn to Appendix B.

Foremost Farms USA is a Midwest dairy cooperative that offers 11 scholarships worth $2,000 each to any of their 1,550 member-owners (and their children).   http://www.foremostfarms.com

The **Midwest Dairy Association** is a nonprofit organization that offers a number of $500 scholarships to dairy producers (who help fund this organization) and their spouses and children. http://www.midwestdairy.com

Related Careers

Agricultural sales and service, dairy construction and equipment contractor, agricultural and food scientist, agricultural worker, and agricultural inspector.

Animal Husbandry Manager

Vital Statistics

Salary: The median wage for a manager of animal husbandry is $36,040, according to 2006 data from the U.S. Bureau of Labor Statistics.

Employment: Opportunities for managers of animal husbandry should increase between 10 and 20 percent over the next five years.

Education: Most individuals in this position need either training in a vocational school, related on-the-job experience, or an associate's degree in a related program.

Work Environment: Managers of animal husbandry often work outdoors, using objects, tools, or machine controls. They may work on a single farm or travel between two or more farms.

If you enjoy eggs for breakfast, a grilled chicken sandwich at lunchtime, or honey-baked ham on your dinner table, give a nod of thanks to the animal husbandry managers who make these meals possible. Animal husbandry, of course, is farming that's concerned with the care and breeding of domestic animals—such as cattle, poultry, hogs, and sheep—so that they can be successfully harvested for food products.

We're talking big business. In 2005, for instance, cattle sales brought farmers over $49 billion. Poultry, including egg production, netted $30 billion in sales, followed by hogs and pigs at $15 billion, and sheep and lambs at $570 million. Today hundreds of thousands of U.S. workers are employed in animal production. Many of them work for, or are self-employed on, small family farms. Only 10 percent of all U.S. farms are corporate farms or large family-owned operations producing more than $250,000 in sales yearly. Yet these agribusinesses account for more than 75 percent of the farm output in the United States.

A growing number of both large corporate farms and small family farmers are joining one of agriculture's fastest growing trends—organic farming. It relies on natural processes and materials to raise animals and plants. These processes include free-range pasturing and natural pesticides and exclude hormone-treated livestock. These days, for instance, farmers in more than 30 states raise certified organic livestock.

Both organic and standard animal husbandry methods call for physically demanding work. Raising animals, unlike growing crops, is a year-round operation. Livestock need to be rotated from one pasture to another. Fences and equipment need to be kept in good repair. Animals need to be inseminated, supervised during the birth process, and checked for disease—though some of these tasks may be subcontracted to specialists. What's more, because of the high cost of animal feed, most farms that produce animals also plant, grow, and harvest crops. Animal husbandry managers know that they can feed their own animals more cheaply by growing crops rather than purchasing commercial feed. Add in the drive for greater and greater efficiency and competition from other U.S. and international animal product producers. It's easy to conclude that being an animal husbandry manager is an occupation best suited to those who are hard-working, determined to succeed, and smart enough to seek out the most profitable opportunities. Such opportunities include niche markets, in which farmers are in direct contact with their customers through farmer's markets, and marketing cooperatives, in which farmers collectively own businesses that process and sell their products.

For all their effort, animal husbandry managers have the satisfaction of knowing that they are producing a product that is healthful, raised in clean, sanitary conditions, in great demand, and that provides many nutritional benefits. What's more, they know that the food they produce helps not only to feed U.S. customers, but also supplies the demand for animal products around the world. International sales of U.S. animal products bring in billions of dollars. So as a side benefit, animal husbandry managers are directly linked to offsetting the U.S. trade deficit.

> **"The key to everything is patience. You get the chicken by hatching the egg—not by smashing it."**
> —Arnold Glasow, poet

On the Job

Above all, animal husbandry managers are responsible for the health and welfare of the animals under their care. They must be able to treat simple injuries, diagnose basic animal illnesses, inseminate livestock, and arrange for the feeding, bedding, transportation, and general care of the livestock they raise. They also must be able to oversee these tasks when others do them.

This includes being able to explain procedures carefully, and make sure instructions are understood and followed properly.

In supervising an animal husbandry operation, managers must also be on guard against many hazards. These include injuries from farm machinery or the misuse of pesticides (which can harm animals as well as people).

They must also be alert to avoid the overuse of fertilizers, which can deplete the soil. A good animal husbandry manager respects the earth's resources and avoids accidents, taking prompt action when mishaps occur in order to minimize damage.

In raising and marketing the animals they produce, animal husbandry managers also use plenty of business skills. Getting a good price for their animals and controlling the costs of their feed and other materials is essential. They also set productions goals, monitor output, hire and fire workers, and arrange credit to tide the farm over until the animals can be sold.

To keep these entrepreneurial skills sharp, animal husbandry managers master computer skills, spreadsheets, and databases. They attend conferences to exchange up-to-date farm knowledge and they make the most of their marketing, finance, and other business classes. Clearly this job requires dedication and stamina. Yet those who choose this occupation enjoy the pleasures of a rural life. The ultimate reward for animal husbandry managers is the satisfaction of producing a crop of healthy animals that will help feed people around the world while still sustaining the earth's natural resources.

Keys to Success

To be a successful animal husbandry manager, you need (a) strong

- desire to work with livestock
- knowledge of breeding, raising, and harvesting animals
- sense of dedication and responsibility
- business know-how
- problem-solving abilities
- managerial skills

Do You Have What It Takes?

Students interested in animal husbandry management should have a genuine love of farming and the business of raising animals. Did you grow up on a farm, have experience working in the farming industry, or enjoy working in an occupation that requires strength and stamina? Then animal husbandry management may be a strong career choice for you. In high school try to gain valuable experience by working on a farm, participating in Future Farmers of America activities, and taking classes in such subjects as agriculture (in states where it is offered), biology, or zoology. You can also arrange to job-shadow an animal husbandry manager to see exactly what the job involves.

A Typical Day at Work

Farming and raising animals is hard but rewarding work. Your day begins around 7 a.m. with spot-checking the cattle for any signs of disease. Helped by family members, you then feed and water the animals. Next you're off to borrow your neighbor's hay wagon to transport straw bales to your barn, where you and your brother break down the bales to use as bedding for your animals. The rest of the morning you spend repairing equipment and doing other maintenance chores. After lunch, you vaccinate the cattle against flu or tracheitis. This is especially important to do before calves are weaned from their mothers. Your day ends with another feeding operation, with a last look at the changing prices for cattle and a quick computation of what your sales will be. With luck, you're home today at 6:30 for dinner.

Your buddy, who works for a large corporate farm, spends her day monitoring the needs of her animals. Additionally she focuses on marketing her farm's products by placing ads in trade journals. She also reaches out to potential new markets through telephone and direct-mail campaigns.

How to Break In

Animal husbandry managers usually take part in almost every aspect of the business, especially on smaller farms. So the more widespread farming experience you have the better your chance of finding a management position. If you've grown up on a family farm and have participated in Future Farmers of America or 4-H programs, so much the better. But the complex nature of farming today makes a two-year associate's degree in agriculture essential. These days it's also almost a basic necessity to arrange an apprenticeship to an experienced farmer. To set one up, speak to your college advisor, ask your personal contacts, or look for leads in trade journals or online (see Career Connections, page 71).

Two-Year Training

Virtually all state university systems have at least one college or school of agriculture, and many offer two-year degrees in animal husbandry. In addition, a survey of U.S. College Search (http://www.uscollegesearch.org) found 40 two-year programs in animal husbandry, mostly at smaller colleges. Students should look for programs that include basic plant and animal science, agricultural economics and business, and courses in agricultural production and marketing. Agriculture programs should also provide computer skills, including database programs and spread sheet programs such as Excel. While taking these classes, students who find they excel in a particular field like mechanics may prefer to work on a larger farm where they can specialize in agricultural equipment repair. Students who find they are more "jacks of all trades" may prefer to work on a smaller farm where they can exercise a full range of their skills.

Although most students who enter an agricultural degree program already have some farm experience, consider supplementing that background with one or more apprenticeships with an experienced farmer. You'll have a chance to put into practice your knowledge and skills in a real-life farming situation.

What to Look For in a School

These are some important questions to ask when looking for a two-year school:

☞ Will the school teach me the skills of managing an animal husbandry operation?

☞ Will the school help me get internships and other job experience?

☞ What kinds of jobs do the school's graduates obtain, and what is the school's job placement rate?

☞ Does the school offer courses in those aspects of animal husbandry that interest me the most?

☞ What are the professors' credentials and experience?

☞ What are the laboratory, model farm, and classroom facilities like? Is the equipment up-to-date?

The Future

The future is looking up for animal husbandry managers. True, some agriculture jobs are being eliminated as farms merge and planting and harvesting procedures are streamlined. However, jobs in animal husbandry management may increase, especially on small-scale operations and on organic farms. In fact, by 2012, 18,000 new employees will be added to the total employment of 52,000 in this job sector.

Did You Know?

More than 15,000 inventions have been patented to improve animal husbandry operations.

Interview with a Professional:
Q&A
Jamey Rauch
Owner and manager, Rauclif Farms, Little Hocking, Ohio

Q: *How did you get started?*

A: I am a seventh generation farmer on the land that my family began farming when they first came to North America. I attended community college to gain knowledge of the business of production. Upon graduation I began raising my own beef animals.

Q: *What's a typical day like?*

A: In the winter, I start the day in the office planning, preparing budgets, and making planting decisions. Then I begin chores in the feed bunk at one barn, feed and check the cows in the pastures, and move to the next barn. I finish around noon, and then take a few hours to make repairs to machinery and order supplies, fertilizer, and seed. We begin afternoon chores around 3:00 p.m., and I am done around 8:00 p.m. In the spring, I spend less time on chores but increase the office time, and begin fieldwork. Summer days I am out of the house by 6:30 a.m. and harvesting wheat, straw, and hay and spraying corn and beans. My wife and children take on some chores while I do the majority of the fieldwork. I am responsible for all of the chemical applications, planting, harvesting, and tillage. Fall is a time of harvest, machinery repairs, and placing orders for next year's cattle.

Q: *What's your advice for those starting a career?*

A: Be patient. Be confident and be willing to learn, change, and move forward. No one can know everything there is to know about agriculture production. Use others as consultants whenever you can. Do not be afraid of technology, but at the same time know your limits.

Q: *What's the best part of managing a farm?*

A: I know that I am the person responsible for the successes as well as the failures I have had. My success comes, I believe, from the fact that I have been willing to listen to others who have the knowledge that I lack.

Job Seeking Tips

✔ Build experience in different areas of agriculture.

✔ Check out what animal husbandry courses are available, especially those that include economics, marketing, and agricultural production.

✔ Decide what aspect of animal husbandry you're interested in and seek relevant experience.

✔ Talk to the career placement office.

✔ Seek out mentors and experienced managers in the field.

Career Connections

For further information, contact the following organizations.

The **Alternative Farming System Information Center National Agricultural Library USDA** http://www.nal.usda.gov/afsic

The **Appropriate Technology Transfer for Rural Areas National Sustainable Agriculture Information Service** http://www .attra.ncat.org

Both of the above organizations supply information on diversified agriculture, education, training, and community-supported agriculture, and the latter specifically publishes information on internships and apprenticeships.

Future Farmers of America http://www.ffa.org

The **Husbandry Institute** is a nonprofit organization dedicated to creating consumer demand for sustainable, ethical animal farming and its products. http://www.husbandryinstitute.org

The **US Department of Agriculture** supplies information on government education and research programs in all aspects of agriculture. http://www.csrees.usda.gov

Associate's Degree Programs

Ohio State University Agricultural Technical Institute, Wooster, Ohio

Barton County Community College, Great Bend, Kansas

Columbia State Community College, Columbia, Tennessee

Delaware Technical & Community College, Owens Campus, Georgetown, Delaware

Laramie County Community College, Cheyenne, Wyoming

Financial Aid

Here are a few agriculture-related scholarships. For more on financial aid for two-year students, turn to Appendix B.

The **CHS Foundation** awards more than $1.7 million annually through grants, scholarships, and educational support to students in the agriculture programs at participating colleges and universities. http://www.chsfoundation.org

The **Monsanto Company** has awarded nearly $1 million in scholarships since 1999 to high school seniors from farm families through the Commitment to Agriculture Scholarship Program. The program is administered by the national Future Farmers of America organization.   http://www.ffa.org

The **National Cattlemen's Foundation** awards twenty $1,500 scholarships each year in conjunction with the Chicago Mercantile Exchange, Inc. to students who are pursuing a career in the beef industry. http://www.nationalcattlemensfoundation.org

Related Careers

Farmer, rancher, agricultural engineer, agricultural and food scientist, and agricultural worker.

Agribusiness Manager

Vital Statistics

Salary: Entry-level agribusiness salaries are typically in the low $30,000s, while the median wage for agribusiness sales representatives is $59,390, according to 2006 figures from the U.S. Bureau of Labor Statistics.

Employment: Employment varies depending on the job and region. Overall, opportunities are expected to grow 10 to 20 percent a year through 2014, with an anticipated need of 182,000 more employees.

Education: Having an associate's degree is an advantage in this field, though not essential. Opportunities to advance, however, are often tied to education.

Work Environment: These jobs often involve working with the public in a store or office setting, but may also involve travel to cultivate potential clients.

The next time you bite into that hamburger, you might stop and think of all the people in agriculture who helped make your meal possible. Besides the cattle farmer, you'd have to include the people who produced, processed, sold, stored, and transported feed for the cattle; produced and sold the seed and fertilizer for the crops used to grow that feed; advertised and marketed that feed, seed, and fertilizer; loaned farmers money to buy equipment or materials; and handled any of their insurance claims. And don't forget the managers of the agricultural cooperatives who purchased those products for the farmer at the best price possible.

Agribusiness is the name we give to all the jobs just mentioned, which manage the processing, transporting, and delivery of food to the consumer; or which provide other services to the people who produce that food. Those jobs include equipment, feed, and agricultural supplies salespersons and store managers, warehouse supervisors, truck drivers, advertising sales agents, marketers, insurance claims adjusters, and loan officers and specialists—just to name the main players. As in any large industry, workers in agribusiness may be salaried employees of companies, self-employed individuals, or workers (usually in sales) who are paid a commission or a percentage of the money generated from the sales they make.

Those in agribusiness who work for larger companies tend to have more specialized jobs. A sales representative for a large company, for example, would be likely to specialize in one product, or group of products, such as fertilizers. An employee of a smaller company, by contrast, may be responsible for selling that company's entire range of products, including seed, feed, fertilizers, and farming equipment.

By helping to arrange the financing, marketing, and selling of the farmer's output, and by selling him essential products such as feed and fertilizer, the agribusiness manager can free up farmers to do what they do best: create, cultivate, and harvest agricultural products. It's possible that in the best circumstances an enterprising beef cattle farmer, for example (see Chapter 8), could do without most of the services provided by agribusiness and be almost completely self-sufficient: He could grow all his own feed crops, recycle his animal and crop waste into fertilizer, share all his equipment with other farmers, and market all his products directly to the consumer. But in today's world, where consumers and producers are usually separated by hundreds of miles, such circumstances are rare. That's why agribusiness managers play a key role in smoothing the way for most farmers to finance, market, and sell their goods at the best price.

On the Job

For the typical agribusiness manager, work involves communicating with fellow employees, customers, or potential customers, either in person or on the phone. This holds true whether he or she supervises employees on a large cooperative or manages business in a retail store, regional sales office, credit union, corporate headquarters, or agricultural storage facility (just to name a few). The purpose of the communication varies widely. It may include assigning production goals to cooperative employees, soliciting orders, demonstrating products or equipment, or persuading customers to switch products. Or it may involve quoting prices or credit terms on products, loans, or services, or consulting with customers concerning the delivery dates or installation related to products or services they have purchased.

Because today's economy is a global one and farms are under pressure to consolidate, farmers face considerable pressure to produce goods as efficiently as possible. This pressure can create anxious individuals. Agribusiness managers must be able to assure their customers that they are there to help and encourage them in their difficult work by offering products and services that will make farming more profitable.

When agribusiness managers are not communicating with employees or customers, they may be planning work or production schedules, preparing reports of business transactions, compiling lists of prospective customers, writing up sales contracts for orders they have already made, or making up lists of prospective customers to call upon.

Do You Have What It Takes?

Think you'd be comfortable developing a marketing plan for selling an agricultural product or working with balance sheets, income statements, and PowerPoint presentations? Then being an agribusiness manager or sales representative may be the job for you. Those who work in this industry should know agriculture, be good at business, mathematics, and science, and grasp basic economics. They should also have the "people skills" to communicate with the wide variety of individuals with whom they interact, including agricultural workers, bank and credit-agency managers, and individual consumers. What's more, they must be able to bring all their skills together to find creative solutions to agribusiness problems.

Keys to Success

To be a successful agribusiness manager, you should have strong
- sales skills
- communication and people skills
- knowledge of farming needs and products
- business and financial basics
- attention to detail
- problem-solving skills
- trustworthiness and perseverance

> "Agricultural careers are very difficult and challenging. There are always new problems to solve and new directions to develop. This gives persons working in this field a great sense of accomplishment as progress is made."
> —Richard A. Sharrer, president, farm-commodities business

How to Break In

The more understanding you have of the various aspects of farming—animal husbandry, crop cultivation, bookkeeping and accounting, equipment maintenance and repair, and so on—the better agribusiness manager you will be, for you must be able to communicate with the people who do these jobs. Growing up on a farm is good preparation for any future agribusiness manager. So is training in business methods and accounting. As always, internships and membership in student organizations and professional organizations with student chapters are excellent ways to build up networking contacts that will prove invaluable when finding a job after graduation. After receiving their A.A.S. (associate of applied science) degrees, beginning agribusiness managers also need to keep up to date with new developments in agriculture in order to have the best chances to enter and advance in their field.

A Typical Day at Work

Agribusiness managers work in such a wide variety of settings, the typical day will also vary widely. However, a common position is that of a traveling sales representative for a major fertilizer manufacturer. Such a "rep" might begin her day around 9 a.m., or whenever the first feed and farm store that she has targeted for the day opens for business. She and the store's buyer might discuss how to promote the various products of her company's that the store carries. She would also answer any questions the buyer may have about new products and takes orders. The sales rep then checks each department in the store to make sure that her company's products are shelved and displayed in a way that will maximize sales. For example, she may suggest that a particular product be displayed at the end of the aisle for greater visibility. She might also work with the buyer on building a new display to promote a product.

Around noon, or whenever her visit is over, she'll take notes on her morning and, if convenient, arrange to meet the next buyer on her route for lunch. Such meetings with one's customers build the rapport that is an essential element of all sales efforts. After lunch, the traveling sales rep repeats her routine in another store or two, again leaving time at the end of each visit to take notes for later reference. Her day might end with an hour or so of office work checking on the status of previously made orders, confirming the next day's visits, and troubleshooting issues that crop up. This might include handling customers who are late paying their bills or dealing with wrong or misplaced orders.

Two-Year Training

Colleges and universities offer a sometimes confusing range of two-year degrees in agribusiness, agricultural business operations, or general agricultural business and management. The options vary widely from institution to institution. Some smaller colleges offer a general A.A.S. degree that includes basic biology, chemistry, math, English, and human behavior. This will be supplemented with electives in such subjects as agriculture chemicals, animal diseases, beef production, and principles of macroeconomics, management, and marketing. Larger universities, such as the State University of New York/Alfred, offer A.A.S. degrees in three specialized programs: farm business management; agricultural sales/retailing management; and agricultural economics and business, with the intent to transfer to a four-year program. Other A.A.S. agribusiness programs, such as the one at Ohio State University/Agricultural Technology Institute, divide the agricultural business degree path into as many as five options: general, crop production, livestock production, horticulture, or food systems. Still other schools offer just two concentrations: farm business management and agricultural sales and retailing management. Students must select from among their options the program that best prepares them to enter the agribusiness specialty that interests them. Their choices include sales and service representative for feed, seed, fertilizer, and equipment industries; inspectors of agricultural products; managers of farm supply stores, feed mills, food retail and whole-sale businesses; sales and management positions in agricultural marketing businesses; and managers of agricultural cooperatives.

What to Look For in a School

These questions can help you find a two-year school that's right for you:

☞ Will the school teach me the basic skills in agribusiness operations or agricultural business management?

☞ Will I learn additional skills in the phase(s) of agriculture that especially interest(s) me?

☞ Will the school be able to help me get internships and apprentice-ships?

☞ What kinds of jobs do the school's graduates land, and what is the school's placement rate?

☞ What are the professors' credentials and experience? Have they worked in the agriculture industry? Are they available outside the classroom and by e-mail?

☞ What are the classrooms and model farm facilities like? Is the equipment up to date?

☞ Is there an agricultural business club or a chapter of a national agribusiness-related organization on campus?

The Future

The projected growth of sales representatives in the agricultural sector, as well as for the agribusiness managers who supervise them, is expected to be average until 2012. There is always a need, however, for talented individuals who have the know-how to serve the agricultural community intelligently and efficiently. As older managers retire or leave the occupation, younger managers will be needed to replace them. Managers and salespersons who are knowledgeable and skilled in meeting the needs of smaller-scale farms will also be in demand.

Interview with a Professional:
Q&A
Richard A. Sharrer

President, Ag Com, Inc., New Oxford, Pennsylvania

Q: *How did you get started?*

A: Ag Com Inc. is an agricultural commodities processing and distribution company that evolved from a family business. As a young person working for my father, I did jobs like shovel feed, drive trucks, and check sick chickens. That hands-on experience, plus my associate's degree, gave me the start I needed.

Q: *What's a typical day like?*

A: Our present operations include feed manufacturing, flour milling, soybean processing, fertilizer manufacture, and commodity trucking and distribution. I am involved in understanding the day-to-day challenges faced by our management team that runs the various divisions. I spend time discussing ways to accomplish and facilitate operations and challenges. For example, each day I monitor market decisions, manufacturing reports, inventories, shipping logs, and cash flows. These data enable me to give our personnel the direction they need to accomplish our goals. I attempt to develop a vision for the best direction for Ag Com, and motivate and challenge everyone to follow. I review results with our team and look for ways to improve our operations.

Q: *What's your advice for those starting a career?*

A: A truly successful person must be able to balance their professional challenges with being a friend and neighbor, a good son or daughter, a great husband or wife, and the best father or mother. Persons starting their career should first have a plan for where they want to go. Without question, honesty, integrity, and loyalty are key components needed to succeed.

Q: *What's the best part of being an agribusiness manager?*

A: Agricultural careers are very difficult and challenging. There are always new problems to solve, challenges to conquer, and new directions to develop. This gives persons working in this field a great sense of accomplishment and satisfaction. I also very much appreciate all the people that I work with because as an industry, we possess people of integrity and commitment.

Did You Know?

For every person employed in agricultural production, there are three persons needed in related agribusiness operations.

Job Seeking Tips

✔ Join organizations and take part in activities where you will meet individuals who can advise you in your career choice.

✔ Decide what you're interested in and seek relevant experience.

✔ Talk to the career placement office.

✔ Seek out and get career advice from those in the field in which you're interested.

✔ See Appendix A for tips on creating a résumé, interviewing for schools or jobs, and collecting references.

Career Connections

Students should contact their state farm bureaus and other agriculture-related state and local agencies for internship and career possibilities. Other career connections include the following:

John Deere, one of the world's largest manufacturers of agricultural equipment, has an internship program for students in Deere-related fields of study, as well as a part-time employment program for students who are in colleges located near John Deere facilities. http://www.deere.com

The **National Agri-Marketing Association** has campus chapters, publishes a magazine, awards scholarships, and provides networking opportunities. http://www.nama.org

Associate's Degree Programs

Here are a few schools offering quality programs in agribusiness/agricultural business operations or general agricultural business and management:

Casper College, Casper, Wyoming

Lord Fairfax Community College, Middletown, Virginia

North Dakota State College of Science, Wahpeton, North Dakota

Pennsylvania State University/Berks-Lehigh Valley College, Reading, Pennsylvania

State University of New York/Alfred, Alfred, New York

Vermont Technical College, Randolph Center, Vermont

Financial Aid

Here are a few agribusiness-related scholarships. For others, check state and local agriculture-related businesses and Appendix B.

Agriliance and Croplan Genetics awards twenty $1,000 scholarships to qualified high school seniors interested in agriculture-related studies.   http://www.agriliance.com

American Agri-Women offers $500 scholarships to farm-raised women and their daughters to take accredited agriculture-related courses.   http://www.americanagriwomen.org

The **United Agribusiness League** awards scholarships to students of agriculture and related fields.   http://www.ual.org

The **United States Department of Agriculture** offers scholarships of $5,750 to groups traditionally underrepresented in the food and agriculture sciences. http://www.usda.gov. Direct e-mails to jgilmore@reeusda.gov.

Related Careers

Advertising sales agent; insurance sales agent; sales representative for mechanical equipment, supplies, and instruments; real estate sales agent; driver/sales worker; purchasing agent, and buyer of farm products.

Wildlife Technician

Vital Statistics

Salary: The average salary for wildlife technicians is $33,250, according to 2006 data from the U.S. Bureau of Labor Statistics.

Employment: The job outlook for environmental professionals is mixed. There are plenty of jobs due to an ongoing concern about the environment. However, these careers are so popular that competition is keen.

Education: A two-year associate's degree is the minimum education requirement to become a wildlife technician. As the job becomes increasingly sophisticated, more training may be necessary.

Work Environment: Wildlife technicians work both indoors and outdoors, usually in district offices as well as state and national parks and wildlife refuges, or private ranches.

Do you sometimes feel you understand animals better than you do humans? Do you own a pet or just like being around animals? Do you enjoy reading books about wildlife? If you answered "yes" to one or more of these questions, then you might consider a career as a wildlife technician.

Wildlife technicians assist biologists and zoologists in protecting and maintaining the wildlife in a specific geographical area. Often this is a national or state park, a wildlife refuge, or some other public land. Wildlife technicians usually report to scientists, and they work for federal, state, and local departments of fish and wildlife. They are also employed by colleges and universities, environmental consulting companies, public utilities, and private employers. Both the work possibilities and the scope of activities for wildlife technicians are quite varied—as is the competition for these highly attractive jobs.

Wildlife technicians work to protect and maintain wildlife. To carry out these goals, they observe wildlife to collect data on their behavior; trap and tag animals to track of their movements; cultivate habitats for wildlife (these consist mainly of plants); and maintain public trails and roads so that humans and wildlife can coexist successfully. Through each of these tasks, wildlife technicians help to preserve the variety of plant and animal life on which every species depends.

Here's how it works: Once an animal species has been identified as endangered or threatened, a scientist, often a biologist in the U.S. Fish and Wildlife Services, writes a recovery plan. A wildlife technician then collects data that help to provide the statistical backing or rationale for this plan. The data may concern the numbers of the species in question or details about their range and other characteristics of the animal's habitat.

About one-third of all American animals and plants appear to be at risk due to human activity, according to the National Wildlife Federation (NWF). However, today, almost 80 percent of the endangered or threatened species have recovery plans, and more than one third of all such species are on the rebound. What's more, of the species on the endangered or threatened list for more than seven years, nearly half are stable or improving. As key figures in preparing wildlife recovery plans, wildlife technicians deserve part of the credit for this amazing progress.

Wildlife technicians also work in a variety of other settings. In all of these, they must collect accurate data and communicate it clearly so that the biologists and zoologists can use it correctly. If the data is sound, then these decision-makers can more successfully balance the needs of both human beings and wildlife and help animals survive and thrive on a planet with limited resources and growing human populations.

On the Job

Wildlife technicians provide services and support to zoologists and biologists in wildlife management and animal biology. The activities of wildlife technicians are quite varied. One week they may conduct surveys to obtain samples of water, soil, animal matter, or plant matter to find out if a particular habitat can support a given species. (These surveys require an eye for detail and accuracy, as the technicians observe the subjects, collect the data, and analyze it.) The next week, in preparation for restocking an area with deer, wildlife technicians may build ponds for water, plant drought-resistant grass crops, and cut down brush that restricts deer movement. Clearly, a technician's ability to work independently and resourcefully is important, since he or she may often work without the assistance of others in remote areas such as canyons which are accessible only by four-wheel drive vehicle. Although wildlife is their focus, direct contact with living creatures is only part of their job. They spend a lot of their time compiling, summarizing, and checking records of wildlife activity. Wildlife technicians may also assist in preparing educational materials that describe their activities, review tax maps and deeds to determine who owns a particular piece of land, and check to see that various landholders have the appropriate agency permits.

> **"Like the resource it seeks to protect, wildlife conservation must be dynamic, changing as conditions change, seeking always to become more effective."**
> —Rachel Carson, author of *Silent Spring*

Keys to Success

To be a successful wildlife technician, you need a strong

- interest in wildlife
- ability to work independently as well as in groups
- love of the outdoors
- ability to communicate well in writing and orally
- drive to work hard and enthusiastically
- eye for detail and good observational skills

Do You Have What It Takes?

As a wildlife technician, you're the advocate for one to dozens of species. How well you do your job has real, important consequences for these animals. You should be dedicated and thorough in your work. You also should feel comfortable doing a wide range of tasks from trapping and tagging animals and waterfowl to surveying the number of animals in a given area. You'll also need to be trained in how to handle different species. Though you'll wear protective gear when you're in direct contact with wildlife, you'll face some element of risk. After all, there's a reason they're called wild animals. You'll also need to be comfortable with physical labor such as maintaining trails, supervising others when necessary, and communicating to the public about your work.

A Typical Day at Work

On a typical day, you might divide your time between outdoor and indoor activity. If you were, for instance, involved in a peregrine falcon survival study, you might spend the morning in the field observing and counting species of falcons. You might also trap a selection of the birds to tag them or attach radio transmitters. In the afternoon you might enter your observations into a computer program or write up a report on your trapping activity.

Depending on the season, you might find your responsibilities changing as well. For instance, you might trap and tag in the summer and focus on computer-based tasks in the winter. In either case, your days would include the unexpected. For example, if you work in an area where humans and wild animals live in close proximity, you may be called upon to deal with a bear that has broken into someone's house or geese that are polluting the local water supply. It's all part of a day's work.

How to Break In

Start preparing yourself early to land a job as a wildlife technician. For instance, in high school take courses in mathematics, biology, environmental studies, and computer applications. Also keep a nature journal in which you record observations of local wildlife, weather, plant life, and other natural phenomena to sharpen your observational skills. Join local conservation clubs and national environment-related organizations, such as the Wildlife Society. Volunteer for a conservation organization, for instance, take part in bird counts sponsored by the Audubon Society, or apply for a paid summer position at the National Park Service, a state park, or other organization that offers these opportunities. Work hard in these paid and volunteer positions and look for ways to distinguish yourself. Your experience and contacts should put you at the head of the line when a paid position opens up.

Two-Year Training

Look for two-year colleges that offer a degree in wildlife technology and wildlife management. The best courses of study reflect the fact that wildlife are part of their larger environment. These curriculums include courses not only on mammals, but also on identifying, caring for, and managing fish and birds and their habitats. Habitat courses should also include the study of forests, individual trees and plants, soils and water; and how to measure these living things. Wildlife technology students usually take courses in map and aerial photo interpretation as well as GPS (global positioning systems) and GIS (geographic information systems) and radio telemetry. Some schools also require courses in surveying.

Of course, being a wildlife technician also requires a basic knowledge of biology, zoology, computers, and mathematics, so these courses are part of the curriculum. So are courses to sharpen written and oral communication skills and, sometimes, research skills. Many schools also offer separate classes in practical techniques such as CPR and firefighting.

As a wildlife technician, it's also essential to understand the impact of people's desire for recreation and its impact on wildlife and habitats. You may take a course on outdoor recreation where you'll grapple with questions such as how to balance the need to preserve and protect wild animals with the desire for outdoor recreation, which may—if not controlled— threaten the survival of these wild animals. To help answer this question, some schools also offer courses in wildlife law and policy.

Many schools also include courses on wildlife management as part of the wildlife technician program. These courses enable students to bring together our knowledge, research, writing, and computer skills to develop a clear grasp of the issues involved in successfully balancing human and wildlife needs.

What to Look For in a School

When considering a two-year school, be sure to ask these questions:

☞ Will the school teach me the basic skills in wildlife technology?

☞ Will I learn additional skills in wildlife technology that interest me?

☞ Will the school assist me in getting internships and apprenticeships?

☞ What kinds of jobs do the school's graduates obtain, and what is the school's job placement rate?

☞ What are the professors' credentials and experience? Have they worked in the wildlife technology field?

☞ What are the classrooms and any associated facilities like? Is the equipment up to date?

☞ Does the school have a wildlife technician club or a student chapter of an organization like the Student Conservation Association?

The Future

Demand for wildlife technicians will be ongoing as threats to endangered species continue. While the competition for these jobs will be great, public awareness of the seriousness of these issues may lead to additional funds becoming available to meet the demand for wildlife technicians' skills.

Did You Know?

Almost 600 species of fish and wildlife—everything from the white abalone (a snail) to the woundfin (a fish)—are endangered or threatened in the United States and its possessions around the world.

Job Seeking Tips

✔ Pursue personal contacts and job opportunities on the Internet, at fish and wildlife agencies, and private sector ranches and preserves.

✔ Talk to the career placement office at your school.

✔ Build a portfolio of your work with a few samples of lab or other reports you've worked on in classes or in paid or volunteer positions.

✔ See Appendix A for tips on creating a résumé, interviewing for schools or jobs, and collecting references.

Interview with a Professional:
Q&A

Rachel Frame
Wildlife technician, Ohio Division of Wildlife,
Athens, Ohio

Q: *How did you get started?*

A: Soon after receiving my A.A.S. degree, I saw a posting on the Internet for a fisheries position. After contacting the fisheries biologist, I learned that the position was filled but I started talking with him anyway. He told me to send in my résumé just in case. He forwarded my résumé to the wildlife department. Within three weeks a wildlife biologist called and asked if I would be interested in a position as a wildlife technician.

Q: *What's a typical day like?*

A: It starts with the realization that I won't be stuck in a cubicle and punching a time clock. Every day offers new learning experiences and challenges. I'm just about to start collecting scientific data on the effects of timber harvesting and prescribed burns [of trees] on reptiles, amphibians, and forest bats. I also educate the public concerning wildlife issues.

Q: *What's your advice for those starting a career?*

A: Become involved in clubs, volunteer with organizations, and make as many connections along the way as possible. Be persistent. A career isn't going to fall in your lap; you need to pursue it. Lastly, be flexible. You may have to move away from a familiar location to pursue your career.

Q: *What's the best part about being a wildlife technician?*

A: It's great to know that the two years I spent in college learning about ecosystems, wildlife behavior, and operation of scientific equipment didn't go to waste. It's even better—deeply comforting, in fact— to know that my assistance in the wildlife field is helping the environment that I deeply love. But the best part of being a wildlife technician is getting to spend my days working around wildlife. There's something about spending time with animals that I find very relaxing.

Career Connections

For more information contact the following organizations.

The **Audubon Society**'s mission is to conserve and restore natural ecosystems, focusing on birds, other wildlife, and their habitats. http://www.audubon.org

The **National Wildlife Federation** sponsors national programs on such issues as endangered species and amphibian decline; and regional programs on species such as the Florida panther and the grizzly bear. The federation lists career opportunities on its Web site. http://www.nwf.org

The **North American Wildlife Technology Association** is a forum for exchanging ideas as well as an accrediting body for wildlife technology programs.   http://www.nawta.org

The **Student Conservation Association** offers three- to 12-month expenses-paid internships in all 50 states with the U.S. Fish and Wildlife Service and state and local agencies and organizations. http://www.thesca.org

The **Wildlife Society** comprises nearly 9,000 wildlife professionals and students and offers great networking opportunities through its TWS-L list server, conferences, and local chapters. http://www.wildlife.org

The **Environmental Career Center** is a fee-based site that lists jobs and conferences.   http://www.environmentalcareer.com.

Associate's Degree Programs

Here are a few schools offering quality wildlife technician programs:

Haywood Community College, Clyde, North Carolina

Hocking College, Nelsonville, Ohio

Pennsylvania State University/DuBois, DuBois, Pennsylvania

Spokane Community College, Spokane, Washington

Zane State College, Zanesville, Ohio

Financial Aid

Here is a sample wildlife-related scholarship. For more on financial aid for two-year students, turn to Appendix B.

The **Future Farmers of America Foundation** awards scholarships in fish and wildlife technology, among other areas.   http://www.ffa.org

Related Careers

Wildlife manager, wildlife enforcement officer, biological technician or aide, park technician or aide, ranger aide, and zoological technologist.

Aquaculture Technician

Vital Statistics

Salary: The median yearly salary for an aquaculture technician is $35,540, according to 2006 data from the U.S. Bureau of Labor Statistics.

Employment: Opportunities for aquaculture technicians are projected to grow at an average rate.

Education: An associate's degree is required for this position, though some candidates may get by with vocational training or on-the-job experience.

Work Environment: Aquaculture technicians usually work outdoors in and around manmade fish ponds, fish tanks, and other controlled water environments.

If you recently ate either trout or a catfish in a restaurant, it was almost certainly raised on a farm rather than caught in the wild. Shrimp or salmon? There's a fifty-fifty chance that either was also farm-raised. Most farm-raised fish are freshwater species like catfish and trout, but saltwater farm-raised fish may dramatically increase in number if laws are changed to allow fish farms as far as 200 miles out into the sea. What's more, many experts consider the aquaculture industry to be the fastest growing sector in agriculture today. By 2035, it is estimated that over half the fish we eat will come from fish farms.

As the world's supply of wild fish gradually dwindles, farm-raised fish are a natural alternative. Farm-raised fish both boost protein output and help feed a growing world population. Of course, with increased farming of fish will come at least two new concerns: pollution caused by raising fish in close quarters, and disease and interbreeding caused when farm-raised fish escape and mix with fish raised in the wild.

In the United States, most farm-raised fish come from the southern states, especially Mississippi, but the industry has now spread nationwide. Today there are more than 4,000 aquaculture facilities, the vast majority of which are small businesses with total sales of less than $250,000.

What is it like to raise fish? In many ways, it's like raising any other living creature. The big difference, of course, is that your stock is raised in water rather than on land. Otherwise, there are many similarities: like any living things, fish have to be born safely, fed properly, and brought up in a space that is clean and spacious enough so that they will eventually grow to their natural size limit.

Aquaculture technicians help prepare fish and fish products for six markets: food, bait, aquariums, fee fishing operations, pond and lake stockings, and biological supply houses. They work at both government-run hatcheries as well as private fish farms. While fish farms focus on raising fish to adulthood, fish hatcheries specialize in the birth and early phases of fish production. In either facility, however, technicians do some of the same tasks: raising stock; feeding fish, monitoring water quality; checking for disease and taking steps to prevent outbreaks; using various meters to measure oxygen, acidity, and salinity levels in the water; and assisting with experiments to test nutritional diets, control parasites, and the like.

Besides having a passion for freshwater or seawater creatures, or both, those who enter the field of aquaculture should enjoy working outside. They should have good communication skills and the ability to work as part of a team. Fishing and boating experience are a plus, but not essential. Successful aquaculture technicians have the career satisfaction of knowing that they are increasing the world's supply of a healthful, essential food product.

> **"If you want to maintain a sustainable supply of fish, you have to farm the fish, rather than mine them."**
> —Maurice Strong, former senior adviser to
> UN Secretary General Kofi Annan

On the Job

Depending on the season of the year, you may be spending most of your day incubating fish eggs, feeding young fish, or trapping and moving older fish from the fish hatchery to lakes, ponds, streams, or commercial tanks. Each of these steps requires different skills. For example, the aquaculture technician incubates trout eggs in special containers called McDonald jars. The technician makes water flow through the jars just fast enough to keep the trout eggs suspended so they receive enough oxygen to grow without flowing out of the jars at the top. With techniques such as this, the aquaculture technician acts as a combination of baby doctor and surrogate mother to fish—helping them to survive from birth through infancy to young adulthood.

Though nature's timetable can sometimes be altered to suit human needs, the sheer numbers of your "babies" (up to half a million fish fry [recently hatched fishes] at the peak of the season in a single fishery) will probably mean long hours of work during hatching and rearing periods. You'll also spend part of your day on other jobs such answering questions from customers. As you advance in the job, you may also find yourself mentoring beginning aquaculturists or educating the public about the joys of fish farming.

Besides raising fish and educating the public, you'll likely also help conduct research regarding your facility's production techniques. For instance, you may help determine why a particular species fails to thrive in a certain location, or what kind of food makes this species reach its optimum size fastest. Then you'll apply what you learn, improving both your knowledge base and, perhaps, your company's bottom line.

Keys to Success

To be a successful aquaculture technician, you need (a) strong
- knowledge of fish care, feeding, and breeding
- emphasis on teamwork
- written and oral communication skills
- talents in working with your hands
- desire to work outdoors

A Typical Day at Work

There are so many kinds of fish that are farmed and so many possible ways to raise and use them that it's hard to generalize about an aquaculture technician's typical day. If you specialize in raising salmon, for instance, your day might begin with testing the water quality in the freshwater tanks where the salmon are being raised and changing the oxygen level if necessary. After feeding the fish you accompany the farm manager on a tour of the facility to observe the young salmon and make sure they are healthy, removing any that appear diseased for later testing. Next you remove any fish wastes and catch a sampling of the young fish to weigh. After lunch, you administer the disease tests and enter the weight data you gathered into your company's database. Based on your weight results, you may spend the afternoon selecting above average-weight fish for transfer to the farm's brood-stock program. In this program, fish are grown to maturity so that eggs and sperm may be harvested from them to grow bigger and better fish. Toward the end of the day, you take a truckload of larger fish to the farm's ocean facility, where they will be placed in cages so they can grow to market size. It may be a long day since, as with many agricultural jobs, Mother Nature often sets your timetable.

Do You Have What It Takes?

Students interested in aquaculture and fisheries should have a special love for all things fish-related. If you enjoy fishing, keep fish in an aquarium, or are just curious to learn about the tremendous variety of species that exist, you may find a career in aquaculture quite fascinating. Of course, if you think of fish as unappetizing creatures, then obviously aquaculture is not for you. But if you are attracted by the grace and beauty of fish and their practical uses as a food source, then being an aquaculture technician can prove an exciting career.

How to Break In

Almost any aquaculture technician will tell you that making as many contacts as possible in the fish farming community (perhaps by volunteering) is the best way to break into this relatively new but fast-growing field. Of course good academic preparation is a necessary foundation on which any career in aquaculture is built. You should enjoy studying science—especially chemistry, biology, and ecology—and be comfortable using computers and working with tools and machines. You should also know your math. In high school don't forget to join programs sponsored by groups like the Future Farmers of America and 4-H. In college you may find similar groups, or you can become a student member of a group like the American Fisheries Society. In these ways you can establish a network of sources for information and jobs.

Two-Year Training

Although only around 22 two-year colleges list aquaculture or fisheries sciences and management as majors, that number is likely to grow as the field becomes larger. The best aquaculture curriculum covers the connections between fish and the rest of the environment. Besides the usual introductory course on fish culture, a good program includes courses on botany, zoology, chemistry, biology, and soil science. To assure that students get hands-on experience in a hatchery or similar setting, all schools require a series of work experiences, arranged by the college. Since farm-raised fish are bred in close quarters, disease is a frequent factor. Therefore fish pathology is usually a required subject too.

In addition to science courses, many two-year degree programs in aquaculture also include courses such as organizational behavior, public law and policy, or economics. Some math and computer courses are typically required. Most schools also offer a course in the business of aquaculture as well as one or more courses in aquaculture management, hatchery maintenance, and technical writing, communications, and speech. Other related subjects include map reading and surveying, statistics, fish genetics and breeding, water supply, and sanitation. Some schools also offer courses in career success or career preparation. Others stress hands-on skills like equipment operation (chain saws, watercraft, and so on) or emergency procedures.

What to Look For in a School

When choosing a two-year school for a career in aquaculture, be sure to ask these questions:

☞ Will the school teach me the basic skills in aquaculture technology and management?

☞ Will I learn additional skills in aquaculture that interest me?

☞ Will the school be able to help me get internships and apprenticeships?

☞ What kinds of jobs do the school's graduates obtain, and what is the school's placement rate?

☞ What are the professors' credentials and experience? Have they worked in the field of aquaculture? Are they available outside the classroom and by e-mail?

☞ What are the classrooms and any associated facilities like? Is the equipment up to date?

☞ Is there an aquaculture club or a student chapter of an organization like the American Fisheries Society on campus?

The Future

The field of aquaculture is likely to expand with the ability to breed additional varieties of fish. Aquaculture is also likely to become more popular as growing populations and the demand for leaner sources of protein increase demand. In addition, the number of sports fishermen (numbering over 63 million in 2000) is expected to expand, and this will lead to a growing number of fish raised for stocking lakes, rivers, and streams. Given all these facts, the future for aquaculture technicians is a rosy one. In fact, the U.S. Department of Labor, which estimated the number of aquaculture employees to be more than 52,000, has projected a need for nearly 18,000 additional employees before 2012.

Did You Know?

There are over 20,000 species of fish in the world, yet fewer than 100 species are farmed or cultured today.

Interview with a Professional:
Q&A

Erin McClymonds

Aquaculture technician, CSI Fish Hatchery,
Twin Falls, Idaho

Q: *How did you get started?*

A: I was introduced to aquaculture through a school-to-work program at my high school. I love being outside, and I chose fisheries because of the large number of fish farms in this area. I liked aquaculture so much I worked in the fishery after graduating while I worked on my two-year degree.

Q: *What's a typical day like?*

A: A typical day starts with cleaning the fish troughs and filling the feeders. Other tasks vary depending on the time of year. We raise trout and Snake River white sturgeon. During spawning season there are lots of eggs and fry to care for. At other times the typical day includes loading a truck to deliver live fish to people who bought them for their private ponds. The day ends with cleaning and feeding one more time before heading home. Hatchery work has been called routine, but I would have to disagree. The fish and the environment are constantly changing. You have a chance to observe the entire life cycle of the fish you are working with, and each life stage requires different care.

Q: *What's your advice for those starting a career?*

A: Just to try it. Hands-on experience is the best way to determine if you picked the right career. It is also a great way to get to know people who already work in the field. If there are no jobs currently available, then volunteer to help on a project or see if you can job shadow.

Q: *What's the best part of being an aquaculture technician?*

A: The best part is the hands-on work. I enjoy going to the hatchery every day and working with the fish. I also really enjoy being outside, and this career allows me to spend the majority of my day outdoors.

Job Seeking Tips

✔ Build a portfolio or résumé that includes examples of your experience in fishing, animal care, science-related jobs, and outdoor recreation.

✔ Join organizations or take part in activities that will help you meet people who can advise you on your career.

✔ Decide whether you want to work in the public sector, as in many fish hatcheries, or in the private sector, as in most large-scale fish farms, and then seek relevant experience and internships.

✔ Talk to the career placement counselor at your school.

✔ See Appendix A for tips on creating a résumé, interviewing for schools or jobs, and collecting references.

Career Connections

For more information contact the following organizations.

The **American Fisheries Society** is dedicated to protecting fish resources and promoting fishery professionals.   http://www.fisheries.org

The **Aquaculture Network Information Center** provides links to information about aquaculture.   http://www. aquanic.org

The **U.S. Fish and Wildlife Service**, enforces and regulates the use of fish and wildlife resources.   http://www. fws.gov

The **National Aquaculture Association** promotes the development of aquaculture in an environmentally responsible manner. http://www. nationalaquaculture.org

The **National Fisheries Institute** is an advocacy organization for all elements of the seafood industry.   http://www. aboutseafood.com

Associate's Degree Programs

Here are a few schools that offer quality aquaculture technician programs:

Carteret Community College, Morehead City, North Carolina

College of Southern Idaho, Twin Falls, Idaho

Hocking College, Nelsonville, Ohio

State University of New York/Morrisville, Morrisville, New York

Trinidad State Junior College, Alamosa, Colorado

Financial Aid

Here is a sample aquaculture-related scholarship. For more on financial aid for two-year students, turn to Appendix B.

Through its Environmental Studies Scholarship Program, **Annie's Homegrown** awards $1,000 scholarships annually to at least 25 students enrolled full time in a two- or four-year program focused on the environmental sciences.

Related Careers

Fishery worker, agricultural inspector, soil conservationist, park naturalist, and forestry technician.

Forest Technician

Vital Statistics

Salary: The average salary of a forest technician is about $34,800, according to 2006 data from the U.S. Bureau of Labor Statistics.

Employment: Jobs for foresters and forest technicians are growing somewhat more slowly than average through 2014. However, new opportunities exist in specialties such as urban forestry and community forestry.

Education: A two-year degree in forest technology is ideal for many employers.

Work Environment: Forest technicians work both in offices and in wooded environments. They may work for public forestland management agencies, private wood-products firms, urban tree-care companies, or nonprofit conservation organizations.

Have you ever climbed a tree and enjoyed the view from your lofty perch? Found refuge from the hot summer sun under the shady branches of a big oak or chestnut? If you have, you've experienced just two of the many ways trees add to our enjoyment of the outdoors. Forest technicians appreciate trees recreational possibilities. They also try to balance those benefits with a respect for the products trees offer. At the same time, they understand the role trees play in preserving healthy ecosystems. For instance, though forest technicians may feel pressure to supply wood for construction of homes and consumer goods, they know they must set limits on the harvesting of wood products. Otherwise, irreplaceable species and habitats can be destroyed.

About half of all forest technicians work on lands that are under the control of the U.S. Forest Service, state forest systems, and other federal and state agencies. These lands make up 193 million acres—an area about the size of Texas. The wood-products industry—including timber and paper producers—employs one quarter of all foresters and forestry technicians. The remaining quarter work as teachers or consultants or in related fields. In all, there's a wide diversity in opportunities for foresters. In fact, the Society of American Foresters lists among its members, more than 700 job categories and almost 14,000 separate employers. By law, U.S. forests are to be managed for multiple uses: "timber, watershed, range, outdoor recreation, and wildlife and fish purposes." With all these possible uses of trees, forest technicians can find just the area that makes use of their particular interests and talents.

Forest technicians perform a range of tasks in looking after the nation's public and private forests. They enforce the laws that govern the use of forests, replant trees after forest destruction by fires and other catastrophic events, assist in logging operations that thin the forest and assure maximum growth of the remaining trees, treat or prevent diseases that infect trees, and show local landowners how to manage their forestland for maximum economic and recreational benefit.

It's hard to imagine our people and environments thriving without the work of foresters and forest technicians who sustains the nation's forests. Without timber, the construction and housing industry would be devastated. Without trees to protect our watersheds, reservoirs would become polluted by the runoff from nearby population centers, farms, and industries. Without trees and other vegetation, our open spaces might soon become dustbowls. By assuring that our forests are properly maintained, forest technicians help preserve our ecosystem, with its delicate balance between human and natural needs. In so doing, forest technicians find huge career satisfaction. They know that their actions have helped to preserve a vital part of the environment for future generations to use and enjoy.

> ## "If a tree dies, plant another in its place."
> — Carl Linnaeus, revolutionary
> eighteenth-century biologist

On the Job

Forest technicians enjoy so many employment possibilities that a person could get lost in the trees, so to speak. A technician could work for a federal, state, and local parks department or environmental protection and conservation agency. Or he or she could find a job in the forest-products industries, in production, sales, and technical services; pulp and paper technology; or in development of new ways to use wood and its byproducts. Technicians might also take advantage of increasing public concern for wildlife to work for an organization that specializes in developing multiple-use plans for forests that focus on wildlife preservation. Finally, they could capitalize on the growing demand for the peace and quiet provided by wild areas by working for a group that specializes in natural resource recreation management.

Forest technicians typically spend a good deal of time literally surrounded by trees—counting, marking, surveying, measuring, or observing their types and characteristics. Their work is a mixture of physical and mental labor. They may physically collect data, for instance, on the effects of acid rain on a particular type of tree. Then they might analyze the data to figure out whether to plant a species that is more acid-rain resistant. Or technicians may assess how much forestland must be preserved to protect an important watershed area.

To do these tasks, technicians use cool tools that can measure everything from the age of a tree to the thickness of growth in a given stand of forest. Yes they also cut down trees, usually with a chain saw. Just as gardens must be pruned, forests must occasionally be thinned to assure the maximum growth of the remaining trees. Sometimes forest technicians must clear (or mark for clearing) whole swaths of trees in order to provide recreation areas for a rising population. Working alone or in groups, forest technicians carry out the plan for a particular forest. Often their goal is to fulfill the "multiple use" policy which guides foresters and forestry officials.

Keys to Success

To be a successful forester, you should have (a) strong

- passion for and understanding of trees and woodlands
- knowledge of geography, biology, geology, and math
- decision-making skills
- communication and listening skills
- manual dexterity and ability to climb and lift, and operate equipment such as chain saws.
- time-management skills.

Do You Have What It Takes?

Future forest technicians should love the outdoors and enjoy working both in nature and with people. They should have a knack for dealing with a problem by analyzing each part of it and coming up with a practical solution. An interest in science, math, and computers is also necessary. Keep in mind that a forest technician may have to call on all these faculties (except maybe the computer skills!) while slogging along a forest trail in a driving rainstorm.

How to Break In

In high school you'll want to take courses in life sciences like biology and physical sciences like chemistry, as well as social sciences like economics and government to prepare yourself for more advanced work in college. It's also a good idea to join school clubs in areas like ecology or conservation where you can build teamwork and leadership skills. Or you can volunteer for service organizations like Landmark Volunteers, environmental groups like the National Resources Defense Council and the Sierra Club, or government agencies like the National Park Service. With this background, you'll be in a good position to successfully pursue paid job opportunities. During the summers look for work with a timber company or a government forest service.

A Typical Day at Work

If you are working as a forest technician for a federal or state agency, your day might start with an outdoor survey of a large forest section, which is slated for brush and deadwood clearance and selective harvesting to create an area that is less fire-prone. In your tour you'll estimate the number of trees that need to be cut down and the approximate volume of the brush and deadwood that needs to be removed. After lunch, you head back to your office, write up your observations, and submit them to a forester who will incorporate them into the master plan for the larger forest district. Later in the day the forester asks you to plan a work detail and assign crew members who will carry out the brush clearance and timber harvest project over the next few days.

Two-Year Training

Colleges and universities that offer two-year programs in forestry, forest sciences, and forest technology can be found across the United States. However, they are less numerous in some parts of the Southwest and Prairie regions, where there are fewer forests. Look for programs recognized by the Society of American Foresters, a professional organization.

Specific courses may include forest products and forest production, ecology, wildlife, and mensuration (how to use geometry to measure lengths, areas, or volumes; how to use trigonometry and algebra to solve problems such as how many trees a given area can support.) Other courses may include communications, statistics, computer applications, and research skills, for instance, to gather data on the size, age, and health of a stand of trees.

One or more internships may be part of the programs. Some schools even maintain their own forests or tree farms. One university states that for every hour of lecture, the student spends two hours in a "living classroom"—the school's tree farm. In most forestry programs you'll find plenty of opportunities for outdoor learning, since topics such as surveying, mapping, tree study, and forest study are best learned by combining classroom study with field experience.

Forest technicians who want to advance further in their education can pursue certificates in specialized areas of forestry. Perhaps the most common of these is the Licensed Professional Forester certification. Requirements vary by state, but generally require passing a written or oral exam; an academic degree; field experience; and professional and character references.

What to Look For in a School

When considering a two-year school, be sure to ask these questions:

☞ Will the school teach me the basic skills in forest technology?

☞ Will I learn additional skills in the areas of forestry that interest me?

☞ Will the school be able to help me get internships and apprenticeships?

☞ What kinds of jobs do the school's graduates land, and what is the school's placement rate?

☞ What are the professors' credentials and experience? Have they worked in the agriculture industry? Are they available outside the classroom and by e-mail?

☞ What are the classrooms and any associated facilities like? Is the equipment up to date?

☞ Is there a forest technician club on campus or a student chapter of a group such as the Society of American Foresters?

The Future

Because of an overall tightening in the number of federal employees in forest-related positions, slower-than-average growth is projected for forest technicians over the next five years or more, especially in the private sector. However, an increased concern about conservation issues like exotic pest control and water resource protection may provide additional employment opportunities. In addition, opportunities for specialists in urban forestry or geographical information systems may be increasing at the state and local level.

Did You Know?

The United States has almost as much forestland today as it had in 1907.

Interview with a Professional: Q&A

Scott Rolfe

Forestry technician and licensed professional forester, New Hampshire Department of Resources, Environment, and Economic Development

Q: *How did you get started?*

A: I grew up on a small farm in New Hampshire, and that instilled a connection in me to natural resources that most people take for granted. But it was not until I was 26 that I knew I needed to change careers from being a food-industry manager. I'm an avid outdoors person, and so I decided to further my education with a forestry degree.

Q: *What's a typical day like?*

A: Some days I may end up bushwhacking three miles or more through the forest with axe and paint in hand doing boundary-line maintenance. Other days I may be walking through a forest and collecting information (or "cruise data") on the trees, laying out temporary pathways used to shuttle logs and trees out of the woods for a timber sale, or checking on an active timber harvest operation. Then again there is a lot of office work to catch up with on inclement days—mapping using data on forests collected by satellite, processing cruise data, and finalizing contracts and records of timber delivered to a timber mill.

Q: *What's your advice for those starting a career?*

A: One of my first supervisors said, "If you keep your nose to the grindstone you will succeed in this business." Going to a good forestry school, striving for a good GPA, getting any experience you can in a particular field, and making contacts with people already in a career you desire will all add up to success.

Q: *What is the best part of about being a forest technician?*

A: Working in the natural landscape and striving to be the best steward of our remaining natural resources for future generations to enjoy is the best part of the job for me.

Job Seeking Tips

✔ Join organizations and take part in activities where you will meet people who can advise you on your chosen career

✔ Decide what aspect of forestry you're interested in—for example, recreational or economic uses of forests, law enforcement of forest regulations, or public education about forests—and seek relevant experience and internships.

✔ Talk to the career placement counselor at your school.

✔ See Appendix A for tips on creating a résumé, interviewing for schools or jobs, and collecting references.

Career Connections

For further information contact the following organizations.

The **American Forest and Paper Association** represents the forest products industry.   http://www.afandpa.org

American Forests is the largest tree-planting conservation organization.   http://www.americanforests.org

The **American Tree Farm System** supports the sustainability of forests, watersheds, and habitats through stewardship by private individuals. http://www.treefarmsystem.org

The **Society of American Foresters** offers information, technical expertise, and networking opportunities for students.   http://www.safnet.org

The **Student Conservation Association** offers expenses-paid internships with the U.S. Park Service and U.S. Forest Service.   http://www.thesca.org

The **USDA Forest Service** is a federal agency that manages over 193 million acres of public lands in national forests and grasslands. http://www.fs.fed.us

Associate's Degree Programs

Here are a few schools offering quality forest technology programs. All are recognized by the Society of American Foresters:

Horry-Georgetown Technical College, Georgetown, South Carolina

Pennsylvania College of Technology, Williamsport, Pennsylvania

Spokane Community College, Spokane, Washington

State University of New York/College of Environmental Science and Forestry, Wanakena, New York

University of New Hampshire, Thompson School of Applied Science, Durham, New Hampshire

Financial Aid

Here are a few forestry-related scholarships. Also check the state chapters of national forestry organizations. For more on financial aid for two-year students, see Appendix B.

The **Council of Eastern Forest Technicians Schools** is a professional organization of 15 academic institutions in the Eastern United States and Canada that offers scholarships to students studying at its member schools.   http://www.cefts.org

The **Forest Products Society** is an international nonprofit technical association that sponsors awards and scholarships through some of its sections and chapters. The Society has a student membership category and campus chapters.   http://www.forestprod.org

The **National Hardwood Lumber Association** awards $1,500 scholarships to individuals to pursue careers in the hardwood industry. http://www.nhla.org

Related Careers

Forestry aide, fire control aide, GIS technician, timber and log buyer, log scaler, log grader, lumber inspector, timber cruiser, logging supervisor, forest surveyor, forest management consultant, lumber yard supervisor, lumber mill manager, forestry equipment and product salesperson, park technician, and conservation aide.

Appendix A
Tools for Career Success

When 20-year-old Justin Schulman started job-hunting for a position as a fitness trainer—his first step toward managing a fitness facility—he didn't mess around. "I immediately opened the Yellow Pages and started calling every number listed under health and fitness, inquiring about available positions," he recalls. Schulman's energy and enterprise paid off: He wound up with interviews that led to several offers of part-time work.

Schulman's experience highlights an essential lesson for jobseekers: There are plenty of opportunities out there, but jobs won't come to you—especially the career-oriented, well-paying ones that that you'll want to stick with over time. You've got to seek them out.

Uncover Your Interests

Whether you're in high school or bringing home a full-time paycheck, the first step toward landing your ideal job is assessing your interests. You need to figure out what makes you tick. After all, there is a far greater chance that you'll enjoy and succeed in a career that taps into your passions, inclinations, and natural abilities. That's what happened with career-changer Scott Rolfe. He was already 26 when he realized he no longer wanted to work in the food industry. "I'm an avid outdoorsman," Rolfe says, "and I have an appreciation for natural resources that many people take for granted." Rolfe turned his passions into his ideal job as a forest technician.

If you have a general idea of what your interests are, you're far ahead of the game. You may know that you're cut out for a health care career, for instance, or one in business. You can use a specific volume of *Top Careers in Two Years* to discover what position to target. If you are unsure of your direction, check out the whole range of volumes to see the scope of jobs available. Ask yourself, what job or jobs would I most like to do if I *already* had the training and skills? Then remind yourself that this is what your two-year training will accomplish.

You can also use interest inventories and skills-assessment programs to further pinpoint your ideal career. Your school or public librarian or guidance counselor should be able to help you locate such assessments. Web sites such as America's Career InfoNet (http://www.acinet.org) and JobWeb (http://www.jobweb.com) also offer interest inventories. Don't forget the help advisers at any two-year college can provide to target your interests. You'll find suggestions for Web sites related to specific careers at the end of each chapter in any *Top Careers in Two Years* volume.

Unlock Your Network

The next stop toward landing the perfect job is networking. The word may make you cringe. But networking isn't about putting on a suit, walking into a roomful of strangers, and pressing your business card on everyone. Networking is simply introducing yourself and exchanging job-related and other information that may prove helpful to one or both of you. That's what Susan Tinker-Muller did. Quite a few years ago, she struck up a conversation with a fellow passenger on her commuter train. Little did she know that the natural interest she expressed in the woman's accounts payable department would lead to news about a job opening there. Tinker-Muller's networking landed her an entry-level position in accounts payable with MTV Networks. She is now the accounts payable administrator.

Tinker-Muller's experience illustrates why networking is so important. Fully 80 percent of openings are *never* advertised, and more than half of all employees land their jobs through networking, according to the U.S. Bureau of Labor Statistics. That's 8 out of 10 jobs that you'll miss if you don't get out there and talk with people. And don't think you can bypass face-to-face conversations by posting your résumé on job sites like Monster.com and Hotjobs.com and then waiting for employers to contact you. That's so mid-1990s! Back then, tens of thousands, if not millions, of job seekers diligently posted their résumés on scores of sites. Then they sat back and waited . . . and waited . . . and waited. You get the idea. Big job sites like Monster and Hotjobs have their place, of course, but relying solely on an Internet job search is about as effective as throwing your résumé into a black hole.

Begin your networking efforts by making a list of people to talk to: teachers, classmates (and their parents), anyone you've worked with, neighbors, worship acquaintances, and anyone you've interned or volunteered with. You can also expand your networking opportunities through the student sections of industry associations (listed at the end of each chapter of *Top Careers in Two Years*); attending or volunteering at industry events, association conferences, career fairs; and through job-shadowing. Keep in mind that only rarely will any of the people on your list be in a position to offer you a job. But whether they know it or not, they probably know someone who knows someone who is. That's why your networking goal is not to ask for a job but the name of someone to talk with. Even when you network with an employer, it's wise to say something like, "You may not have any positions available, but might you know someone I could talk with to find out more about what it's like to work in this field?"

Also, keep in mind that networking is a two-way street. For instance, you may be talking with someone who has a job opening that isn't appropriate for you. If you can refer someone else to the employer, either person may well be disposed to help you someday in the future.

Dial-Up Help

Call your contacts directly, rather than e-mail them. (E-mails are too easy for busy people to ignore, even if they don't mean to.) Explain that you're a recent graduate in your field; that Mr. Jones referred you; and that you're wondering if you could stop by for 10 or 15 minutes at your contact's convenience to find out a little more about how the industry works. If you leave this message as a voicemail, note that you'll call back in a few days to follow up. If you reach your contact directly, expect that they'll say they're too busy at the moment to see you. Ask, "Would you mind if I check back in a couple of weeks?" Then jot down a note in your date book or set up a reminder in your computer calendar and call back when it's time. (Repeat this above scenario as needed, until you get a meeting.)

Once you have arranged to talk with someone in person, prep yourself. Scour industry publications for insightful articles; having up-to-date knowledge about industry trends shows your networking contacts that you're dedicated and focused. Then pull together questions about specific employers and suggestions that will set you apart from the job-hunting pack in your field. The more specific your questions (for instance, about one type of certification versus another), the more likely your contact will see you as an "insider," worthy of passing along to a potential employer. At the end of any networking meeting, ask for the name of someone else who might be able to help you further target your search.

Get a Lift

When you meet with a contact in person (as well as when you run into someone fleetingly), you need an "elevator speech." This is a summary of up to two minutes that introduces who you are, as well as your experience and goals. An elevator speech should be short enough to be delivered during an elevator ride with a potential employer from the ground level to a high floor. In it, it's helpful to show that 1) you know the business involved; 2) you know the company; 3) you're qualified (give your work and educational information); and 4) you're goal-oriented, dependable, and hardworking. You'll be surprised how much information you can include in two minutes. Practice this speech in front of a mirror until you have the key points down very well. It should sound natural though, and you should come across as friendly, confident, and assertive. Remember, good eye contact needs to be part of your presentation as well as your everyday approach when meeting prospective employers or leads.

Get Your Résumé Ready

In addition to your elevator speech, another essential job-hunting tool is your résumé. Basically, a résumé is a little snapshot of you in words, reduced to one 8½ x 11-inch sheet of paper (or, at most, two sheets). You need a résumé whether you're in high school, college, or the workforce, and whether you've never held a job or have had many.

At the top of your résumé should be your heading. This is your name, address, phone numbers, and your e-mail address, which can be a sticking point. E-mail addresses such as sillygirl@yahoo.com or drinkingbuddy @hotmail.com won't score you any points. In fact they're a turn-off. So if you dreamed up your address after a night on the town, maybe it's time to upgrade. (Similarly, these days potential employers often check Myspace sites, personal blogs, and Web pages. What's posted there has been known to cost candidates a job offer.)

The first section of your résumé is a concise Job Objective (e.g., "Entry-level agribusiness sales representative seeking a position with a leading dairy cooperative"). These days, with word-processing software, it's easy and smart to adapt your job objective to the position for which you're applying. An alternative way to start a résumé, which some recruiters prefer, is to rework the Job Objective into a Professional Summary. A Professional Summary doesn't mention the position you're seeking, but instead focuses on your job strengths (e.g., "Entry-level agribusiness sales rep; strengths include background in feed, fertilizer, and related markets and ability to contribute as a member of a sales team"). Which is better? It's your call.

The body of a résumé typically starts with your Job Experience. This is a chronological list of the positions you've held (particularly the ones that will help you land the job you want). Remember: never, never any fudging. However, it is okay to include volunteer positions and internships on the chronological list, as long as they're noted for what they are.

Next comes your Education section. Note: It's acceptable to flip the order of your Education and Job Experience sections if you're still in high school or have gone straight to college and don't have significant work experience. Summarize the major courses in your degree area, any certifications you've achieved, relevant computer knowledge, special seminars, or other school-related experience that will distinguish you. Include your grade average if it's more than 3.0. Don't worry if you haven't finished your degree. Simply write that you're currently enrolled in your program (if you are).

In addition to these elements, other sections may include professional organizations you belong to and any work-related achievements, awards, or recognition you've received. Also, you can have a section for your interests, such as playing piano or soccer (and include any notable achievements regarding your interests, for instance, placed third in Midwest Regional Piano Competition). You should also note other special abilities, such as "Fluent in French" or "Designed own Web site." These sorts of activities will reflect well on you, whether or not they are job-related.

You can either include your references or simply note, "References upon Request." Be sure to ask your references permission to use their name and alert them to the fact that they may be contacted, before you include them on your résumé. For more information on résumé writing, check out Web sites such as http://www.resume.monster.com.

Craft Your Cover Letter

When you apply for a job either online or by mail, it's appropriate to include a cover letter. A cover letter lets you convey extra information about yourself that doesn't fit or isn't always appropriate in your résumé. For instance, in a cover letter, you can and should mention the name of anyone who referred you to the job. You can go into some detail about the reason you're a great match, given the job description. You also can address any questions that might be raised in the potential employer's mind (for instance, a gap in your résumé). Don't, however, ramble on. Your cover letter should stay focused on your goal: to offer a strong, positive impression of yourself and persuade the hiring manager that you're worth an interview. Your cover letter gives you a chance to stand out from the other applicants and sell yourself. In fact, 23 percent of hiring managers say a candidate's ability to relate his or her experience to the job at hand is a top hiring consideration, according to a Careerbuilder.com survey.

You can write a positive, yet concise cover letter in three paragraphs: An introduction containing the specifics of the job you're applying for; a summary of why you're a good fit for the position and what you can do for the company; and a closing with a request for an interview, contact information, and thanks. Remember to vary the structure and tone of your cover letter. For instance, don't begin every sentence with "I."

Ace Your Interview

Preparation is the key to acing any job interview. This starts with researching the company or organization you're interviewing with. Start with the firm, group, or agency's own Web site. Explore it thoroughly; read about their products and services, their history, and sales and marketing information.

Check out their news releases, links that they provide, and read up on or Google members of the management team to get an idea of what they may be looking for in their employees.

Sites such as http://www.hoovers.com enable you to research companies across many industries. Trade publications in any industry (such as *Food Industry News, Hotel Business,* and *Hospitality Technology*) are also available online or in hard copy at many college or public libraries. Don't forget to make a phone call to contacts you have in the organization to get an even better idea of the company culture.

Preparation goes beyond research, however. It includes practicing answers to common interview questions:

☞ *Tell me about yourself* (Don't talk about your favorite bands or your personal history; give a brief summary of your background and interest in the particular job area.)

☞ *Why do you want to work here?* (Here's where your research into the company comes into play; talk about the firm's strengths and products or services.)

☞ *Why should we hire you?* (Now is your chance to sell yourself as a dependable, trustworthy, effective employee.)

☞ *Why did you leave your last job?* (This is not a talk show. Keep your answer short; never bad-mouth a previous employer. You can always say something simply such as, "It wasn't a good fit, and I was ready for other opportunities.")

Rehearse your answers, but don't try to memorize them. Responses that are natural and spontaneous come across better. Trying to memorize exactly what you want to say is likely to both trip you up and make you sound robotic.

As for the actual interview, to break the ice, offer a few pleasant remarks about the day, a photo in the interviewer's office, or something else similar. Then, once the interview gets going, listen closely and answer the questions you're asked, versus making any other point that you want to convey. If you're unsure whether your answer was adequate, simply ask, "Did that answer the question?" Show respect, good energy, and enthusiasm, and be upbeat. Employers are looking for people who are enjoyable to be around, as well as good workers. Show that you have a positive attitude and can get along well with others by not bragging during the interview, overstating your experience, or giving the appearance of being too self-absorbed. Avoid one-word answers, but at the same time don't blather. If you're faced with a silence after giving your response, pause for a few seconds, and then ask, "Is there anything else you'd like me to add?" Never look at your watch or answer your cellphone during an interview.

Near the interview's end, the interviewer is likely to ask you if you have any questions. Make sure that you have a few prepared, for instance:

☞ *"Tell me about the production process."*

☞ *"What's your biggest short-term challenge?"*

☞ *"How have recent business trends affected the company?"*

☞ *"Is there anything else that I can provide you with to help you make your decision?"*

☞ *"When will you make your hiring decision?"*

During a first interview, never ask questions like, "What's the pay?" "What are the benefits?" or "How much vacation time will I get?"

Find the Right Look

Appropriate dressing and grooming is also essential to interviewing success. For business jobs and many other occupations, it's appropriate to come to an interview in a nice (not stuffy) suit. However, different fields have various dress codes. In the music business, for instance, "business casual" reigns for many jobs. This is a slightly modified look, where slacks and a jacket are just fine for a guy, and a nice skirt and blouse and jacket or sweater are acceptable for a woman. Dressing overly "cool" will usually backfire.

In general, watch all of the basics from the shoes on up (no sneakers or sandals, and no overly high heels or short skirts for women). Also avoid attention-getting necklines, girls. Keep jewelry and other "bling" to a minimum. Tattoos and body jewelry are becoming more acceptable, but if you can take out piercings (other than in your ear), you're better off. Similarly, unusual hairstyles or colors may bias an employer against you, rightly or wrongly. Make sure your hair is neat and acceptable (get a haircut?). Also go light on the makeup, self-tanning products, body scents, and other grooming agents. Don't wear a baseball cap or any other type of hat; and by all means, take off your sunglasses!

Beyond your physical appearance, you already know to be well bathed to minimize odor (leave your home early if you tend to sweat, so you can cool off in private), make good eye contact, smile, speak clearly using proper English, use good posture (don't slouch), offer a firm handshake, and arrive within five minutes of your interview. (If you're unsure of where you're going, "Mapquest" it and consider making a dry-run to the site so you won't be late.) First impressions can make or break your interview.

Remember Follow-Up

After your interview, send a thank you note. This thoughtful gesture will separate you from most of the other candidates. It demonstrates your ability to follow through, and it catches your prospective employer's attention one more time. In a 2005 Careerbuilder.com survey, nearly 15 percent of 650 hiring managers said they wouldn't hire someone who failed to send a thank you letter after the interview. Thirty-two percent say they would still consider the candidate, but would think less of him or her.

So do you hand write or e-mail the thank you letter? The fact is that format preferences vary. One in four hiring managers prefer to receive a thank you note in e-mail form only; 19 percent want the e-mail, followed up with a hard copy; 21 percent want a typed hard-copy only; and 23 percent prefer just a handwritten note. (Try to check with an assistant on the format your potential employer prefers.) Otherwise, sending an e-mail and a handwritten copy is a safe way to proceed.

Winning an Offer

There are no sweeter words to a job hunter than, "We'd like to hire you." So naturally, when you hear them, you may be tempted to jump at the offer. *Don't.* Once an employer wants you, he or she will usually give you some time to make your decision and get any questions you may have answered. Now is the time to get specific about salary and benefits, and negotiate some of these points. If you haven't already done so, check out salary ranges for your position and area of the country on sites such as Payscale.com, Salary.com, and Salaryexpert.com (basic info is free; specific requests are not). Also, find out what sorts of benefits similar jobs offer. Then don't be afraid to negotiate in a diplomatic way. Asking for better terms is reasonable and expected. You may worry that asking the employer to bump up his offer may jeopardize your job, but handled intelligently, negotiating for yourself in fact may be a way to impress your future employer—and get a better deal for yourself.

After you've done all the hard work that successful job-hunting requires, you may be tempted to put your initiative into autodrive. However, the efforts you made to land your job—from clear communication to enthusiasm—are necessary now to pave your way to continued success. As Danielle Little, a human-resources assistant, says, "You must be enthusiastic and take the initiative. There is an urgency to prove yourself and show that you are capable of performing any and all related tasks. If your manager notices that you have potential, you will be given additional responsibilities, which will help advance your career." So do your best work on the job, and build your credibility. Your payoff will be career advancement and increased earnings.

Appendix B

Financial Aid

One major advantage of earning a two-year degree is that it is much less expensive than paying for a four-year school. Two years is naturally going to cost less than four, and two-year graduates enter the workplace and start earning a paycheck sooner than their four-year counterparts.

The latest statistics from the College Board show that average yearly total tuition and fees at a public two-year college is $2,191, compared to $5,491 at a four-year public college. That cost leaps to more than $21,000 on average for a year at a private four-year school.

With college costs relatively low, some two-year students overlook the idea of applying for financial aid at all. But the fact is, college dollars are available whether you're going to a trade school, community college, or university. About a third of all Pell Grants go to two-year public school students, and while two-year students receive a much smaller percentage of other aid programs, the funding is there for many who apply.

How Does Aid Work?

Financial aid comes in two basic forms: merit-based and need-based.

Merit-based awards are typically funds that recognize a particular talent or quality you may have, and they are given by private organizations, colleges, and the government. Merit-based awards range from scholarships for good writing to prizes for those who have shown promise in engineering. There are thousands of scholarships available for students who shine in academics, music, art, science, and more. Resources on how to get these awards are provided later in this chapter.

Need-based awards are given according to your ability to pay for college. In general, students from families that have less income and fewer assets receive more financial aid. To decide how much of this aid you qualify for, schools look at your family's income, assets, and other information regarding your finances. You provide this information on a financial aid form—usually the federal government's Free Application for Federal Student Aid (FAFSA). Based on the financial details you provide, the school of your choice calculates your Expected Family Contribution (EFC). This is the amount you are expected to pay toward your education each year.

Once your EFC is determined, a school uses this simple formula to figure out your financial aid package:

Cost of attendance at the school
- – Your EFC
- – Other outside aid (private scholarships)
- = Need

Schools put together aid packages that meet that need using loans, work-study, and grants.

Know Your School

When applying to a school, it's a good idea to find out their financial aid policy and history. Read over the school literature or contact the financial aid office and find out the following:

✔ *Is the school accredited?* Schools that are not accredited usually do not offer as much financial aid and are not eligible for federal programs.

✔ *What is the average financial aid package at the school?* The typical award size may influence your decision to apply or not.

✔ *What are all the types of assistance available?* Check if the school offers federal, state, private, or institutional aid.

✔ *What is the school's loan default rate?* The default rate is the percentage of students who took out federal student loans and failed to repay them on time. Schools that have a high default rate are often not allowed to offer certain federal aid programs.

✔ *What are the procedures and deadlines for submitting financial aid?* Policies can differ from school to school.

✔ *What is the school's definition of satisfactory academic progress?* To receive financial aid, you have to maintain your academic performance. A school may specify that you keep up at least a C+ or B average to keep getting funding.

✔ *What is the school's job placement rate?* The job placement rate is the percentage of students who find work in their field of study after graduating.

You'll want a school with a good placement rate so you can earn a good salary that may help you pay back any student loans you have.

Be In It to Win It

The key to getting the most financial aid possible is filling out the forms, and you have nothing to lose by applying. Most schools require that you file the FAFSA, which is *free* to submit, and you can even do it online. For more information on the FAFSA, visit the Web site at http://www.fafsa.ed.gov. If you have any trouble with the form, you can call 1-800-4-FED-AID for help.

To receive aid using the FAFSA, you must submit the form soon after January 1 prior to the start of your school year. A lot of financial aid is delivered on a first-come, first-served basis, so be sure to apply on time.

Filing for aid will require some work to gather your financial information. You'll need details regarding your assets and from your income tax forms, which include the value of all your bank accounts and investments. The form also asks if you have other siblings in college, the age of your parents, or if you have children. These factors can determine how much aid you receive.

Three to four weeks after you submit the FAFSA, you receive a document called the Student Aid Report (SAR). The SAR lists all the information you provided in the FAFSA and tells you how much you'll be expected to contribute toward school, or your Expected Family Contribution (EFC). It's important to review the information on the SAR carefully and make any corrections right away. If there are errors on this document, it can affect how much financial aid you'll receive.

The Financial Aid Package

Using information on your SAR, the school of your choice calculates your need (as described earlier) and puts together a financial aid package. Aid packages are often built with a combination of loans, grants, and work-study. You may also have won private scholarships that will help reduce your costs.

Keep in mind that aid awarded in the form of loans has to be paid back with interest just like a car loan. If you don't pay back according to agreed upon terms, you can go into *default*. Default usually occurs if you've missed payments for 180 days. Defaulted loans are often sent to collection agencies, which can charge costly fees and even take money owed out of your wages. Even worse, a defaulted loan is a strike on your credit history. If you have a negative credit history, lenders may deny you a mortgage, car loan, or other personal loan. There's also financial incentive for paying back on time—many lenders will give a 1 percent discount or more for students who make consecutive timely payments. The key is not to borrow more than you can afford. Know exactly how much your monthly payments will be on a loan when it comes due and estimate if those monthly payments will fit in your future budget. If you ever do run into trouble with loan payments, don't hesitate to contact your lender and see if you can come up with a new payment arrangement—lenders want to help you pay rather than see you go into default. If you have more than one loan, look into loan consolidation, which can lower overall monthly payments and sometimes lock in interest rates that are relatively low.

The Four Major Sources of Aid

U.S. Government Financial Aid

The federal government is the biggest source of financial aid. To find all about federal aid programs, visit http://www.studentaid.fed.gov or call 1-800-4-FED-AID with any questions. Download the free brochure *Funding Education Beyond High School*, which tells you all the details on federal programs. To get aid from federal programs you must be a regular student working toward a degree or certificate in an eligible program. You also have to have a high school diploma or equivalent, be a U.S. citizen or eligible non-citizen and have a valid Social Security number (check http://www.ssa.gov for info). If you are a male aged 18–25, you have to register for the Selective Service. (Find out more about that requirement at http://www.sss.gov or call 1-847-688-6888.) You must also certify that you are not in default on a student loan and that you will use your federal aid only for educational purposes.

Some specifics concerning federal aid programs can change a little each year, but the major programs are listed here and the fundamentals stay the same from year to year. (Note that amounts you receive generally depend on your enrollment status—whether it be full-time or part-time.)

Pell Grant

For students demonstrating significant need, this award has been ranging between $400 and $4,050. The size of a Pell grant does not depend on how much other aid you receive.

Supplemental Educational Opportunity Grant (SEOG)

Again for students with significant need, this award ranges from $100 to $4,000 a year. The size of the SEOG can be reduced according to how much other aid you receive.

Work-Study

The Federal Work-Study Program provides jobs for students showing financial need. The program encourages community service and work related to a student's course of study. You earn at least minimum wage and are paid at least once a month. Again, funds must be used for educational expenses.

Perkins Loans

With a low interest rate of 5 percent, this program lets students who can document the need borrow up to $4,000 a year.

Stafford Loans

These loans are available to all students regardless of need. However, students with need receive *subsidized* Staffords, which do not accrue interest while you're in school or in deferment. Students without need can take *unsubsidized* Staffords, which do accrue interest while you are in school or in deferment. Interest rates vary but can go no higher than 8.25 percent. Loan amounts vary too, according to what year of study you're in and whether you are financially dependent on your parents or not. Students defined as independent of their parents can borrow much more. (Students who have their own kids are also defined as independent. Check the exact qualifications for independent and dependent status on the federal government Web site http://www.studentaid.fed.gov.)

PLUS Loans

These loans for parents of dependent students are also available regardless of need. Parents with good credit can borrow up to the cost of attendance minus any other aid received. Interest rates are variable but can go no higher than 9 percent.

Tax Credits

Depending on your family income, qualified students can take federal tax deductions for education with maximums ranging from $1,500 to $2,000.

AmeriCorps

This program provides full-time educational awards in return for community service work. You can work before, during, or after your postsecondary education and use the funds either to pay current educational expenses or to repay federal student loans. Americorps participants work assisting teachers in Head Start, helping on conservation projects, building houses for the homeless, and doing other good works. For more information, visit http://www.americorps.gov

State Financial Aid

All states offer financial aid, both merit-based and need-based. Most states use the FAFSA to determine eligibility, but you'll have to contact your state's higher education agency to find out the exact requirements. You can get contact information for your state at http://www.bcol02.ed.gov/Programs/EROD/org_list.cfm. Most of the state aid programs are available only if you study at a school in the state where you reside. Some states are very generous, especially if you're attending a state college or university. California's Cal Grant program gives needy state residents free tuition at in-state public universities.

School-Sponsored Financial Aid

The school you attend may offer its own loans, grants, and work programs. Many have academic- or talent-based scholarships for top-performing students. Some two-year programs offer cooperative education opportunities where you combine classroom study with off-campus work related to your major. The work gives you hands-on experience and some income, ranging from $2,500 to $15,000 per year depending on the program. Communicate with your school's financial aid department and make sure you're applying for the most aid you can possibly get.

Private Scholarships

While scholarships for students heading to four-year schools may be more plentiful, there are awards for the two-year students. Scholarships reward students for all sorts of talent—academic, artistic, athletic, technical, scientific, and more. You have to invest time hunting for the awards that you might qualify for. The Internet now offers many great scholarship search services. Some of the best ones are:

The College Board (http://www.collegeboard.com/pay)

FastWeb! (http://www.fastweb.monster.com)

MACH25 (http://www.collegenet.com)

Scholarship Research Network (http://www.srnexpress.com)

SallieMae's College Answer (http://www.collegeanswer.com)

Note: Be careful of scholarship-scam services that charge a fee for finding you awards but end up giving you nothing more than a few leads that you could have gotten for free with a little research on your own. Check out the Federal Trade Commission's Project ScholarScam (http://www.ftc.gov/bcp/conline/edcams/scholarship).

In your hunt for scholarship dollars, be sure to look into local community organizations (the Elks Club, Lions Club, PTA, etc.), local corporations, employers (your employer or your parents' may offer tuition assistance), trade groups, professional associations (National Electrical Contractors Association, etc.), clubs (Boy Scouts, Girl Scouts, Distributive Education Club of America, etc.), heritage organizations (Italian, Japanese,

Chinese, and other groups related to ethnic origin), church groups, and minority assistance programs.

Once you find awards you qualify for, you have to put in the time applying. This usually means filling out an application, writing a personal statement, and gathering recommendations.

General Scholarships

A few general scholarships for students earning two-year degrees are

Coca-Cola Scholars Foundation, Inc.
Coca-Cola offers 350 thousand-dollar scholarships (http://www.coca colascholars.org) per year specifically for students attending two-year institutions.

Phi Theta Kappa (PTK)
This organization is the International Honor Society of the Two-Year College. PTK is one of the sponsors of the All-USA Academic Team program, which annually recognizes 60 outstanding two-year college students (http://scholarships.ptk.org). First, Second, and Third Teams, each consisting of 20 members, are selected. The 20 First Team members receive stipends of $2,500 each. All 60 members of the All-USA Academic Team and their colleges receive extensive national recognition through coverage in *USA TODAY*. There are other great scholarships for two-year students listed on this Web site.

Hispanic Scholarship Fund (HSF)
HSF's High School Scholarship Program (http://www.hsf.net/scholar ship/programs/hs.php) is designed to assist high school students of Hispanic heritage obtain a college degree. It is available to graduating high school seniors who plan to enroll full-time at a community college during the upcoming academic year. Award amounts range from $1,000 to $2,500.

The Military
All branches of the military offer tuition dollars in exchange for military service. You have to decide if military service is for you. The Web site http://www.myfuture.com attempts to answer any questions you might have about military service.

Lower Your Costs

In addition to getting financial aid, you can reduce college expenses by being a money-smart student. Here are some tips.

Use Your Campus

Schools offer perks that some students never take advantage of. Use the gym. Take in a school-supported concert or movie night. Attend meetings and lectures with free refreshments.

Flash Your Student ID

Students often get discounts at movies, museums, restaurants, and stores. Always be sure to ask if there is a lower price for students and carry your student ID with you at all times. You can often save 10 to 20 percent on purchases.

Budget Your Funds

Writing a budget of your income and expenses can help you be a smart spender. Track what you buy on a budget chart. This awareness will save you dollars.

Share Rides

Commuting to school or traveling back to your hometown? Check and post on student bulletin boards for ride shares.

Buy Used Books

Used textbooks can cost half as much as new. Check your campus bookstore for deals and also try http://www.eCampus.com and http://www.bookcentral.com

Put Your Credit Card in the Freezer

That's what one student did to stop overspending. You can lock your card away any way you like, just try living without the ease of credit for awhile. You'll be surprised at the savings.

A Two-Year Student's Financial Aid Package

Minnesota State Colleges and Universities provides this example of how a two-year student pays for college. Note how financial aid reduces his out-of-pocket cost to about $7,000 per year.

Jeremy's Costs for One Year

Jeremy is a freshman at a two-year college in the Minnesota. He has a sister in college, and his parents own a home but have no other significant savings. His family's income: $42,000.

College Costs for One Year

Tuition	$3,437
Fees	$388
Estimated room and board*	$7,200
Estimated living expenses**	$6,116
Total cost of attendance	*$17,141*

Jeremy's Financial Aid

Federal grants (does not require repayment)	$2,800
Minnesota grant (does not require repayment)	$676
Work-study earnings	$4,000
Student loan (requires repayment)	$2,625
Total financial aid	*$10,101*
Total cost to Jeremy's family	*$7,040*

* Estimated cost reflecting apartment rent rate and food costs. The estimates are used to calculate the financial aid. If a student lives at home with his or her parents, the actual cost could be much less, although the financial aid amounts may remain the same.

** This is an estimate of expenses including transportation, books, clothing, and social activities.

Index